Jacques-Marie L. Monsabré

Marriage

Conferences delivered at Notre Dame, Paris - Translated from the French by M. Hopper

Jacques-Marie L. Monsabré

Marriage

Conferences delivered at Notre Dame, Paris - Translated from the French by M. Hopper

ISBN/EAN: 9783337188146

Printed in Europe, USA, Canada, Australia, Japan

Cover: Foto ©Lupo / pixelio.de

More available books at **www.hansebooks.com**

MARRIAGE.

CONFERENCES
DELIVERED AT
NOTRE DAME, PARIS.

BY

VERY REV. PÈRE MONSABRÉ, O.P.

Translated from the French,
BY
M. HOPPER.

With the Author's Special Permission.

NEW YORK, CINCINNATI, CHICAGO:
BENZIGER BROTHERS,
Printers to the Holy Apostolic See.
1890.

Nihil Obstat.

        H. A. BRANN, D.D.

Imprimatur.

        ✠ MICHAEL AUGUSTINE,
                Archbishop of New York.

NEW YORK, January 8, 1890.

PREFACE.

THE fame of Father Monsabré as a pulpit-orator is world-wide. He holds the same place to-day in the school of sacred oratory that Father Lacordaire held, and like the illustrious panegyrist of O'Connell, he has filled the first pulpit of the Church in France.

The Lenten conferences in the Cathedral of Notre Dame, Paris, have been preached by Père Monsabré since 1872 with singular success. They are remarkable for learning and piety, and have had a large circulation in France and Italy. The conferences on "Marriage" have an ever-present interest, and the following translation of them will afford the English-speaking world an opportunity to read the best thoughts of the greatest of modern preachers on Marriage, Divorce, etc.

CONTENTS.

CONFERENCE	PAGE
I. THE SANCTITY OF MARRIAGE,	7
II. THE CONJUGAL TIE,	35
III. DIVORCE,	61
IV. LEGISLATION ON MARRIAGE,	88
V. PROFANATION OF MARRIAGE,	115
VI. CELIBACY AND VIRGINITY,	138
INDEX OF THE PRINCIPAL ERRORS CONTRARY TO THE DOGMAS SET FORTH IN THIS VOLUME,	169
ANALYTICAL TABLE OF CONTENTS,	223

Conference I.

The Sanctity of Marriage.

My Lord[1] and Gentlemen:—There is no need of my announcing to you the subject on which I must speak this year. You know it. In the interesting study of the grace of Jesus Christ which has engaged us for five years, there is only one more sacrament for us to examine. It is marriage, the second of the social sacraments, ordained for the reparation of the losses which Christian society suffers from the blows of death, and for the education of the holy race of the children of God.

As the natural family is the foundation of all civil society, so the Christian family is the foundation of that great spiritual society which is collected, governed, and made perfect by the priesthood. The source of the natural family is the conjugal union of man and woman, but in order to make that union the source of the Christian family, God has transferred it from the world of nature to the world of grace, by raising it to the dignity of a sacrament.

This, gentlemen, is an important fact. It will serve as a principle to determine clearly the condition of those united under the law of grace, and to refute the errors of those who pretend to reduce

[1] Monseigneur Richard, Archbishop of Paris.

marriage to the condition of a profane thing and to deliver it up to the sacrilegious caprices of human legislation.

Allow me to make a preliminary declaration in order to clear myself beforehand from the accusations of those who, after having heard me, may see in me only a critic. No one respects human laws more than I do, but this respect is subordinate to my reverence for divine truth and eternal justice. If human laws contradict these two sacred principles, it is not I who revolt against them, it is not I who condemn them: it is truth, it is justice, of which I am an apostle, and which no fear shall ever make me betray.

The subjects of which we shall treat during this short course of sermons are: the sanctity of marriage, the conjugal tie, divorce, legislation on marriage, the profanation of marriage. We shall finally speak of the states of celibacy and virginity, those most delicate, most pure, and most glorious ornaments of society, of which marriage prepares the members.

To-day we shall consider the sanctity of marriage in its primitive institution by God, the Creator of humanity, and in its exaltation by Christ, the author of the sacraments.

My Lord, I have received too kind and too precious encouragements from the place where Your Grace to-day presides over this large and distinguished assembly, not to offer to the venerable prelate who gave them to me the public homage of my sincere regret and of my filial gratitude.

One thing alone consoles me for his absence, namely, to continue, under the auspices of Your Grace, the work which your venerable predecessor confided to me; for I am sure to receive from your paternal heart the same kindness and affection, and from your sacred hands the same blessing.

I.

After having established the foundations of the earth and ordered its elements, God resolved to adorn it, and created those living agencies to whom He gave the command to increase and multiply: *Crescite et multiplicamini.*[1] This short epithalamium inaugurated universal marriages in the plains and in the air, on the mountains and in the depths of the sea. It preceded the appearance of humanity by a long epoch. Discreet hymens of flowers in the depths of their scented corollas, loving meetings of living creatures, who move about seeking for companions to propagate their species in new families. This union of pairs and this multiplication of life is full of venerable mystery, because God has put in it something of His own infinite power and eternal vitality. In obedience to the divine command, individuals form the completion each of the other, in order to become one single principle of life. Partners of the fecundity of God, they perpetuate that which must perish, and prolong through time and space the efficaciousness of the act of creation.

---

[1] Gen. i. 22.

This mystery, gentlemen, grows with life. God had adorned the earth only to prepare it to receive its king. He calls him from within Himself: "Let us make man," He says: *Faciamus hominem;* let us make him to be master: *Faciamus ut præsit;*[1] and He makes him after His own image and likeness, so great, so beautiful, so perfect, that all living creatures shall come by and by to his feet, shall recognize his dominion and receive from him their appropriate names.[2] Man has all that is needful in order to command, and yet God pronounces that it is not good for him to remain alone, and that He must make him a help like unto himself: *Non est bonum esse hominem solum; faciamus ei adjutorium simile sibi.*[3]

I have already told you, gentlemen, when we were studying the origin of humanity, that man should imitate the principle of his being, the tendency of which is to communicate itself, because he cannot keep to himself all the germs of life which God has placed within him. According to the profound reflection of St. Thomas, the high functions of human intelligence should not be sacrificed to the lower functions, whence the life of the body springs; therefore "a help" is needful for man, in whom all the passive power of parentage shall reside, while he, as sovereign dispenser, retains all the active strength. "Therefore let us make for man," said the Lord, " a help

---

[1] Gen. i. 26.
[2] Ibid. ii. 19, 20.
[3] Ibid. ii. 18.

like unto himself:" *Faciamus ei adjutorium simile sibi.* [1]

Whence shall come this help? From the dust from which man sprang? No! Man would cease to be, like God, the only and first principle of the life of his race if the human being to be united to him were not taken from his side. "Sleep, My son," said God, "sleep." And under the influence of a divine magnetism, Adam, lying down on the flowers of Paradise, is overcome by a mysterious sleep, during which God takes away one of his ribs, reclothes it with flesh, and makes for this part of animate man another soul, woman, the charming and chaste spouse of the slumberer. [2]

All astonished at the life she has just received woman waits. ...... To the marriage! to the marriage! King of the world, awake! Adam awakes. He beholds with his eyes her whom he has seen in a prophetic dream, and understands that in her shall be accomplished his perfection. He is intelligence, she is love; he is thought, she is sentiment; he is majesty, she is grace; he is strength, she is gentleness; he is command, she is influence; he is the sower of life, she is the fertile earth where life shall germinate. He admires her, he is softened, he is inflamed, and from his heart, filled with a new love, bursts forth the celebrated epithalamium which reveals to the world of the future the essence and the holy laws of mar-

[1] Cf. *Exposition of Catholic Dogma,* conference 26: *Humanity in Adam,* part I.
[2] Gen. ii. 21, 22.

riage: "This is bone of my bones and flesh of my flesh. She shall be called Woman, because she was taken out of man. Wherefore a man shall leave father and mother, and shall cleave to his wife, and they shall be two in one flesh."[1] To this cry of love God replies by a blessing whence humanity springs, and which submits to man's dominion the creatures which He has already blessed and multiplied: "Increase and multiply, and fill the earth, and subdue it, and rule over" all that it contains: *Crescite et multiplicamini et replete terram, et subjicite eam, et dominamini* ...[2]

Such was the first marriage, the typical marriage. I beg you to consider well its essence, for to this fundamental truth are allied those important questions of rights and duties of which we shall presently speak.

According to current opinion, the essence of marriage consists in the exchange of two free acts by which a man and a woman give themselves each to the other, in order to reproduce their own life, to create a family, and to perfect themselves mutually in one common life. I am not afraid of making a mistake when I affirm that, whilst taking into account the blessings of the Church, to which you attribute the virtue of giving a sacred character to the conjugal union, the greater number of

---

[1] Hoc nunc os ex ossibus meis, et caro de carne mea. Hæc vocabitur Virago, quoniam de viro sumpta est. Quamobrem relinquet homo patrem suum et matrem, et adhærebit uxori suæ, et erunt duo in carne una.—Gen. ii. 23, 24.

[2] Ibid. i. 28.

you have no other idea of marriage. It is a pure and simple contract, of which the whole essence consists in the reciprocal act of the giving and accepting of persons. Allow me to tell you, there is an error in this.

Assuredly, marriage is a contract, but a contract which in no way resembles other human contracts. It is the most exalted, the most venerable, I would almost say, the most extraordinary of contracts. What man therein transmits is not one of those subordinate benefits which are the accessories of his person or of his life; it is not his field, his house, his flock, his fortune, his labor, his services, the fruit of his intelligence and industry; it is himself, his own person, his living person, and with his person, the benefits which depend upon and are allied to it, and on his person, the most delicate and intimate rights.

Man has dared to lay hands on his fellow-man. Abusing his strength, he has seized on human lives powerless to defend themselves against his brutality: he has created slavery. "They are mine," said he formerly of the miserable creatures whom he enslaved to serve his wants, his greed, his caprices, his passions, and his vices. "Mine!" ferocious and sacrilegious cry, which recalls the saddest days of humanity. "Mine!" Oh, no! Man has not the right to say that of another man. Two beings alone can say one to the other, "thou art mine," because they have freely and entirely given themselves to each other.—Thou art mine! I am thine!—it is the cry which thrilled through Eden when the father and mother of the human race were married under the eye of God.

Man and woman give themselves to each other by the exchange of their will and consent. But why? Is it only in order to obey the divine command which wills that the creative act, of which humanity is the issue, should be indefinitely prolonged throughout the ages? Is it only for the happiness of seeing themselves live again in the offspring which resembles them? Is it only for the honor of preserving in the bosom of human society a centre of life on which its existence and strength depend? No, the multiplication of species is an honor to marriage, but it is to a far higher, more delicate and intimate benefit that the conjugal union tends. This benefit is the intermingling of two lives to form one; the mutual perfecting of these lives each by the other. It is the union of mind and heart: *Cor unum et anima una.* It is one disposition giving or imprinting on the other that wherein it is weak, natural qualities moderating and balancing each other, virtues communicated from one to the other in harmonious degrees.

All these perfections are for the benefit of the husband and the wife who acquire them, and still more for the benefit of the children whom they shall bring up after having given them life. To the material birth succeeds a birth far more noble and in more need of care: the birth of an intellectual, moral, and religious life. To this work the two perfected lives of man and woman apply their virtue; and this work is the sublime end of their contract. We can learn from the manner in which the contract is carried out the influence of the motive which decided the union of will and consent. Between man, woman, and child there is a fellowship of love, which love alone has been able to found.

Not that love which belongs merely to the senses, a blind and passing passion that fades as soon as it is satisfied, but the love of the heart, of a wise heart, illuminated by reason, of a heart which is not foolishly smitten with ephemeral charms, that the eyes alone can enjoy, but which seeks in respect and esteem the seat of a faithful and lasting attachment.

Such is the matrimonial contract in its object, its end, its intention. It makes one understand the difference between the two benedictions by which God communicates His fecundity to living things. To plants and animals He says only, "Increase and multiply:" *Crescite et multiplicamini.* It is sufficient. The immovable and silent flower allows the fertile dust which shall reproduce it to fall, or itself unconsciously appropriates it; the animal obeys the unerring laws of instinct which impel it to seek a companion; its fecundity is the result of a brute companionship, and its transient union in no way changes its nature. But to man and woman, who use their reason and their heart in the choice of the being to whom they unite their life; to man and woman, who freely and entirely give themselves to each other; to man and woman, who know themselves to be participators in the work of God; to man and woman, who comprehend the great honor of parentage; to man and woman, who are perfected and communicate their perfection in conjugal society; to man and woman, who are not united like the creatures of an inferior species, but who marry—to them God owed an ampler and more glorious benediction. God had already raised the human pair to the summit of nature; He now adds the empire of the world to the promise of fecundity and to the commandment of reproduction: "Increase and multiply, and fill the earth, and subdue it, and rule over the fishes of the sea, and the fowls of the air, and all living creatures that move upon the earth:" *Crescite, et multiplicamini, et replete terram, et subjicite eam, et dominamini piscibus maris, et volatilibus cœli, et universis animantibus, quæ moventur super terram.*[1] Such was the worthy consecration of that venerable and extraordinary contract the object of which is so precious, the end so noble, the motive so pure and so sweet.

Nevertheless, this contract is not the very essence of marriage. If theologians have called marriage a contract, it is in order to declare its cause,[2] and not to determine its essence. You ask, what, then, is its essence? Listen well and understand fully, for we are now laying down a principle of supreme importance for the whole of our doctrine on matrimony. The essence of marriage is the union, the obligation, the tie resulting from per-

---

[1] Gen. i. 28.

[2] *Causa matrimonii regulariter est mutuus consensus per verba de præsenti expressa.*—Conc. Flor.

fect mutual consent.[1] Marriage has been defined by law "to be the marital union of man and woman between legitimate persons, holding them bound together in one common life": *viri et mulieris conjunctio maritalis, inter legitimas personas, individuam vitæ consuetudinem retinens.* This definition has passed from law into theology, and from theology into the typical catechism, where we should seek the pure idea of Christian dogma.[2] It is the legal and scholastic translation of the poetic effusion of our first parent when he exclaimed: "A man shall leave father and mother and shall cleave to his wife, and they shall be two in one flesh": *Et erunt duo in carne una.*

You will say to me, no doubt, that from perfect mutual agreement there results an obligation, a tie, and that it is sufficient to determine the essence of marriage, if we are content to call it a contract. Pardon me, no, it is not sufficient, for the tie which is the result of the matrimonial contract is not the same as that which is the result of other contracts.

[1] St. Thomas says of the matrimonial union that it is made *ad modum obligationis in contractibus materialibus* (Supp. quæst. 45, a. 2). But this union is marriage itself: *conjunctio potest accipi pro ipsa relatione quæ est matrimonium* (Ibid. quæst. 48, a. 5, ad. 2).—Docendum est, quamvis hæc omnia in perfecto matrimonio insint, consensus videlicet interior, pactio externa verbis expressa, obligatio et vinculum quod ex pactione efficitur, et conjugum copulatio, qua matrimonium consummatur ; *nihil horum tamen matrimonii vim et rationem habere, nisi obligationem istam, et nexum qui conjunctionis vocabulo appellatur.* —Catechism. Trid., part 2, De matrimonii sacramento, no. 5.

[2] Institut. i. 9; Magist. Sent.; Catechism. Conc. Trid., loc. cit.

In human agreements, obligation is to some extent confounded with consent, because it absolutely depends upon it. All the customary contracts of social life: sales, exchanges, leases, service, bequests, and the like, can be cancelled at the will of those who made them. For a contract to be broken and for its obligation to cease, it is sufficient that the wills which had agreed in one sense should then agree in an opposite sense.[1] It is not so in the matrimonial contract. The man and the woman who marry give themselves each to the other, but this gift, once made, depends no longer on mutual agreement. The united pair will say in vain, we were deceived, life to both of us is a burden too heavy for our weary shoulders; let us withdraw from our agreement. They cannot withdraw, for they are united, not by the strength of their wills alone, but by a mysterious power, which has seized them, bound them together in a common life, and on which henceforth they depend. This mysterious power is the very hand of God, the author of our nature, giving to the conjugal union a religious and sacred character in which men can change nothing.[2] This character is not an accidental addition to the contract. It arises from the contract itself; it is the special

---

[1] *Quæ consensu contrahuntur contrario consensu dissolvuntur.* This is, says Pothier, a principle common to all mutual contracts.—*Contract of Marriage* (*Espousals,*) part 2, chap. vii.

[2] Conjunctio potest accipi pro ipsa relatione, quæ est matrimonium, et talis semper est a Deo.—*Summ. Theol.* supp., quæst. 48, a. 2, ad. 2.

mark which distinguishes and separates it from all human contracts.¹ Marriage is holy in its first institution: "it is so by its own strength and nature, and of itself," says a memorable encyclical: *Matrimonium est sua vi, sua natura, sua sponte sacrum.*" ² Antiquity bears witness to this sanctity. Consult its monuments, study the manners and institutions of the nations best governed and most skilled in the knowledge of law and justice, and you will see, as by a kind of anticipation of the mysteries of the future, marriage appear under the form of an act permeated with religion and sanctity, and the nuptials consecrated by ceremonies of worship, by the authority of pontiffs and the ministry of priests; so great has been the power of the voice of nature, of the remembrance of our origin, and of the conscience of the human race even on the souls whom revelation has not enlightened. *Ita magnam in animis cœlesti doctrina carentibus vim habuit natura rerum, memoria originum, conscientia generis humani.* ³

Gentlemen, it is the Sovereign Pontiff Leo XIII.

---

¹ Inest in eo sacrum et religiosum quiddam, non adventitium, sed ingenitum, non ab hominibus acceptum, sed natura insitum.—Leonis XIII. Encyclic. *Arcanum divinæ sapientiæ.*

² Ibid.

³ Testantur et monumenta antiquitatis et mores atque instituta populorum qui ad humanitatem magis accesserant, et exquisitiore juris et æquitatis cognitione præstiterant: quorum omnium mentibus informatum anticipatumque fuisse constat, ut cum de matrimonio cogitarent, forma occurreret rei cum religione et sanctitate conjunctæ. Hanc ob causam nuptiæ apud illos non sine cæremoniis religionum, auctoritate pontificum, ministerio sacerdotum fieri sæpe consueverunt. Ita magnam, etc.—Ibid.

who has just spoken. His infallible authority reminds us that nature has made marriage a holy thing, a thing more holy still if we consider the dignity of the sacrament.

II.

The divine institution of marriage had for its end, not only the reproduction of human nature in its species, but also a perpetuation of a race holy as the pair who should beget it. We can conjecture what it would have been in a state of innocence, if we remember the original perfection of our first parents. The nobleness, majesty, and grace of their bodies, the complete harmony of line, feature, tone, and movement, moulded by God Himself, and animated with a breath of life which manifests itself through an immaculate flesh, radiates on a royal brow, and makes us admire in its virginal beauty the double expansion of grace and of a perfect nature. A body free from the humiliating servitude of matter and giving up to a contemplative life the leisure of a full expansion; a soul illumined with divine knowledge, sensitive to the touch of grace, accustomed to the visits and love of God, invested with sovereign empire over the creatures of this world. Happy pair, bound by an unquenchable love in a place of delights, and for whom all is holy, even in the flesh whose chaste nakedness they behold without blushing, of whose rebellion and criminal pleasures they are ignorant; venerable stock and most pure offspring which they beget without shame and pain, and to whom they communicate as a birthright the integrity and privileges of their sanctified nature.[1] Who can express the joys and glories of this union!

Alas! these joys and glories have passed like a dream. The union of our first parents was not long what God had made it. Man by disobedience frustrated the designs of his Creator, and gave a mortal wound to his nature, the effects of which should be felt by all his race. Marriage did not cease to be a divine thing, and was long respected in the traditions of humanity, but against the sacred recollections transmitted from age to age the passions of fallen nature plotted a universal conspiracy. They obtained the mastery, and the holy laws of marriage were soon everywhere despised. God, to punish woman, had overwhelmed her with the weight of this terrible curse: *Sub viri potestate eris, et ipse dominabitur tui:*[2] "thou shalt be under thy husband's power, and he shall have dominion over thee." Awful to say, man has abused this divine curse even to the most abominable excesses of injustice and cruelty. Chaste love and the oaths of Paradise, he forgot them all. Woman was no longer the inseparable companion of his life, for whom he should leave all, the help who asked of him an undivided heart, bone of his bones with whom he should make but one flesh. He appeared as a sensual and implacable despot,

---

[1] Cf. *Exposition of Catholic Dogma*, conference 26: *Humanity in Adam*, part 2.

[2] Gen. iii. 16.

multiplying unions, assembling around him many women, repudiating, selling, giving, exchanging, treating as a slave the mother of his children. No decent pen would dare relate all the dishonors of the conjugal union amongst the gentiles.

God had separated from the gentiles a people who were to give their blood to the Deliverer Whom the world expected. Guardians of the sacred traditions of humanity, they honored marriage more than other nations, and yet, because of the hardness of their hearts, which rendered them capable of staining the domestic hearth with bloody acts of violence, God relaxed the ties of the primitive institution, and they, abusing this indulgence, took liberties which the rigorous formalities of the law were unable to restrain, and which tended to assimilate their manners with those of the heathen.

The divine institution of marriage was everywhere assaulted, and threatened to crumble to the dust. It was time that a God came to restore it. Behold Him! He enters the world by the ineffable and eternal marriage of His infinite nature with ours, and among all the reparations which He meditates and undertakes, He does not forget that of conjugal society. During the early days of His public life He is present at a wedding and honors it by the first of His miracles;[1] a miracle figurative of the wonderful transformation He desires to work in the union between man and woman. At His command, water changes into wine; at His

---

[1] St. John ii. 1-11.

command, natural marriage, already holy, becomes a sacred sign among things divine, becomes a source of grace, a sacrament.[1] He does not yet declare His design; and when interrogated by the Pharisees on the delicate question of divorce, He escapes from their entanglements by leading them back to the primitive institution of marriage. "Have ye not read," He said, "that He Who made man from the beginning made them male and female? And He said: For this cause shall a man leave father and mother and shall cleave to his wife, and they two shall be in one flesh. Therefore they are not two, but one flesh." *Ita-*

---

[1] Per hoc ergo Dominus invitatus venit ad nuptias, ut conjugalis castitas servaretur et ostenderetur sacramentum nuptiarum.—S. Aug., Tract. ix. *in Joan.* no. 2.

Christus ipse cum discipulis suis invitatus venit [ad nuptias] non tam epulaturus, quam ut miraculum faceret, ac præterea generationis principium sanctificaret, quod ad carnem nimirum attinet. Conveniebat enim, ut qui naturam ipsam hominis renovaturus erat, non solum iis, qui jam in ortum vocati erant, benedictionem impertiretur, sed et iis quoque, qui postea nascituri essent, gratiam præstitueret, et eorum ortum sanctum efficeret:

Κεκλημένος δὲ Χριστὸς καὶ αὐτὸς τοῖς οἰκείοις συναφικνεῖται μαθηταῖς θαυματουργήσων μᾶλλον, ἤπερ ἑστιασόμενος, ἔτι τε πρὸς τούτῳ καὶ αὐτὴν ἁγιάσων τῆς ἀνθρώπου γενεσέως τὴν ἀρχήν· ὅσον δὲ ἧκεν εἰς τὴν σάρκα, φαμέν. Ἔδει γὰρ αὐτὴν τὴν ἀνθρώπου φύσιν ἀνακεφαλαιούμενον, καὶ ὅλην ἀνασκευάζοντα πρὸς τὸ ἄμεινον, μὴ μόνον τοῖς ἤδη πρὸς τὸ ὑπάρξαι κεκλημένοις διανέμειν τὴν εὐλογίαν, ἀλλὰ καὶ τοῖς ὅσον οὐδέπω τεχθησομένοις προευτρεπίζειν τὴν χάριν, καὶ ἁγίαν αὐτῶν καταστῆσαι τὴν εἰς τὸ εἶναι πάροδον.—S. Cyrillus Alex. *Comment. in Joan.*, lib. ii. cap. ii., v. 1. opp. ed. Paris, 1568, tome ii., p. 155.

que jam non sunt duo sed una caro. And He sends them away with this grave and profound reflection: "What, therefore, God hath joined together let no man put asunder." *Quod Deus conjunxit homo non separet.*[1]

To those who know how to meditate and to understand, this saying is full of importance. It is more than a protestation against the disorders which dishonor marriage. There is in it the promise of a grace which shall exalt the divine institution, by introducing it into the sacred hierarchy of supernatural causes. The apostles, the intimate companions of Christ, understood it thus. The doctrine of matrimony which they taught by word of mouth St. Paul has handed down in one of his immortal epistles for the instruction of all Christian generations. Listen to it, gentlemen: "Let women be subject to their husbands, as to the Lord. Because the husband is head of the wife: as Christ is the head of the Church: He is the saviour of His body. Therefore, as the Church is subject to Christ, so also let the wives be to their husbands in all things. Husbands, love your wives, as Christ also loved the Church, and delivered Himself up for it, that He might sanctify it, cleansing it by the laver of water in the word of life, that He might present it to Himself a glorious Church, not having spot or wrinkle, or any such thing, but that it should be holy and without blemish. So also ought men to love their wives as their own bodies. He that loveth his

---

[1] St. Matt. xix. 3–6.

wife, loveth himself. For no man ever hated his own flesh, but nourisheth and cherisheth it, as also Christ doth the Church. Because we are members of His body, of His flesh, and of His bones. For this cause shall a man leave his father and mother, and shall cleave to his wife, and they shall be two in one flesh. This is a great sacrament: but I speak in Christ and in the Church." [1]

Let heresy deal as subtilely as she will with these words of St. Paul, she cannot efface from history the interpretation which has been given to them by the holy Fathers. It will not hinder good sense from believing in the transformation and exaltation of marriage when it is seen to be compared in the apostolic teaching to the mysterious and typical union between Christ and His Church. This text of the Apostle is full of ineffable mystery: mystery in the union between Christ and His Church; mystery in the union between man and woman. And these are the two

---

[1] Mulieres viris suis subditæ sint, sicut Domino; quoniam vir caput est mulieris, sicut Christus caput est ecclesiæ; ipse salvator corporis ejus. Sed sicut ecclesia subjecta est Christo, ita et mulieres viris suis in omnibus. Viri, diligite uxores vestras, sicut et Christus dilexit ecclesiam, et seipsum tradidit pro ea, ut illam sanctificaret, mundans lavacro aquæ in verbo vitæ, ut exhiberet ipse sibi gloriosam ecclesiam, non habentem maculam, aut rugam, aut aliquid hujusmodi, sed ut sit sancta et immaculata. Ita et viri debent diligere uxores suas ut corpora sua. Qui suam uxorem diligit, seipsum diligit. Nemo enim unquam carnem suam odio habuit; sed nutrit et fovet eam, sicut et Christus ecclesiam. Quia membra sumus corporis ejus, de carne ejus et de ossibus ejus. Propter hoc relinquet homo patrem et matrem suam, et adhærebit uxori suæ; et erunt duo in carne una. Sacramentum hoc magnum est, ego autem dico in Christo et in ecclesia.—Ephes. v. 22–32.

unions which the Apostle calls a great sacrament: *Sacramentum hoc magnum est.*[1] The one would not be the type, nor the other the faithful copy, the symbol, the sign, if there was not, in this as in that, a sanctifying virtue. Neither would the man love his wife as Christ loves the Church, nor the wife love her husband as the Church loves Christ, without a grace which purifies, ennobles, and makes love supernatural. Christ, by giving Himself to His Church, sanctifies it; man and woman,

---

[1] Idipsum per allegoriam in Christo interpretatur et in Ecclesia; ut Adam Christum, et Eva præfiguraret Ecclesiam.—Scio quia locus iste ineffabilibus plenus sit sacramentis, et divinum cor quærat interpretis.—S. Hieron. *Comment. in Epist. ad Ephes.*, lib. iii., cap. v.

Quod si lex sancta est, sanctum est matrimonium. Mysterium ergo ad Christum et Ecclesiam ducit apostolus: Ἁγίου δὲ ὄντος τοῦ νόμου ἅγιος ὁ γάμος. Τὸ μυστήριον τοίνυν τοῦτο εἰς τὸν Χριστὸν καὶ τὴν Ἐκκλησίαν ἄγει ὁ Ἀπόστολος.—Clem. Alex., lib. iii. *Strom.*, tome i.

Mysterii sacramentum grande in unitate viri ac mulieris esse significat.—Int. opp. S. Ambros., in append. *in Ep. ad. Ephes.*

Hoc enim mysterium, inquit divus Paulus, magnum est eo quod omnis qui agglutinatur uxori ambo unum corpus sunt. "Τὸ μυστήριον γάρ τοῦτο, φησι, μέγα ἐστι" καθὼς εἶπεν ὁ μακάριος Παῦλος, ὅτι πᾶς ὁ κολλώμενος τῇ γυναικὶ ἓν σῶμα εἰσὶν ἀμφότεροι.—S. Athanas., lib. *De Virginitate*, n. 2, tome ii.

Revera mysterium est, et magnum mysterium, relicto eo qui genuit, eo qui aluit, etiam ea quæ peperit, quæ misere et cum labore parturivit, adhærere virum illi quæ antea neque visa sit: atque hanc omnibus præferre: Ὄντως γὰρ, ὄντως μυστήριόν ἐστι, καὶ μέγα μυστήριον, ὅτι τὸν φύντα, τὸν γεννησάμενον, τὸν ἀναθρεψάμενον, τὴν ὠδινήσασαν, τὴν ταλαιπωρηθεῖσαν ἀφεὶς. . . . τῇ μηδὲ ὀφθείσῃ, μηδὲ κοινόν τι ἐχούσῃ πρὸς αὐτὸν προσκολλᾶται, καὶ πάντων αὐτὴν προτιμᾷ.—S. Chrys., Homil. xx. *in Epist. ad Ephes.*, n. 4.

in giving themselves to each other, ought mutually to sanctify each other. And this is why marriage is a great sacrament: *Sacramentum hoc magnum est.*

Besides, gentlemen, if even in this place the authority of the Apostle should be disputed, it must be admitted in the universal and constant tradition of the Church, which is and only can be an echo of apostolic doctrine. Now, according to the language of tradition, " marriage is a union sealed with the blessing of God." [1]

It is not sufficient that the persons jointly consent and give themselves to each other; the author of grace must intervene. By virtue of His intervention the union is both sanctifying and sanctified. [2] Divine grace penetrates and strengthens it by tightening the bonds. [3]

---

[1] Quod (matrimonium) Ecclesia conciliat, et confirmat oblatio, et obsignat benedictio.—Tertul., lib. ii., *Ad Uxorem*, cap. viii.
Nam quod in ipsa conjunctione connubii a sacerdote benedicatur, hoc est a Deo primo in ipsa conjunctione hominis factum est.—S. Isidor Hispal., *De origine Eccles.*, lib. ii., cap. xix.

[2] Neque vero nos negamus sanctificatum a Christo esse conjugium. —S. Ambros., *Epist. ad Siricum Papam*, n. 5.
Bonum nuptiarum per omnes gentes, atque omnes homines in causa generandi est in fide castitatis; quod autem ad populum Dei pertinet, etiam in sanctitate sacramenti.—S. Aug., *De bono conjugali*, cap. xxiv., n. 32.

[3] Si ergo ratum est apud Deum matrimonium hujusmodi, cur non et prospere cedat, ut pressuris, et angustiis, et impedimentis, et inquinamentis non ita lacessatur, habens jam ex parte divinæ gratiæ patrocinium.—Tertul. lib., *Ad Uxor.*, cap. vii.
Cognoscimus veluti præsulem custodemque conjugii esse Deum, qui non patitur alterum thorum pollui; et si qui fecerit peccare eum in Deum, cujus legem violat gratiam solvat; et ideo quia in Deum

It is a sacrament;[1]—and in Christian marriages the sanctity of the sacrament is more important than the fecundity of the womb: *In christianis nuptiis plus valet sanctitas sacramenti quam fœcunditas uteri.*[2]

A sacrament! We see this word written in all the councils, the liturgies, and in all sacramentaries. Eastern heresies and the great Greek schism did not efface it. It resounds in all the theological schools of the middle ages; we scarcely find in the crowd of the masters of sacred science an original scholastic who is doubtful about its meaning.[3] After this, gentlemen, let Luther deny the transformation worked by Christ in marriage; let Calvin assert that to marry, to labor, to make shoes, are things no more sacred one than the other; let legislators endeavor to reduce marriage to the condition of a purely profane contract; it is indeed high time after fifteen centuries of a teaching which has never varied and which refers to Christ Himself the sanctification of Christian marriage. The Council of Trent was right when it said:

peccat, sacramenti cœlestis amittit consortium.—S. Ambros., lib. i., *De Abraham*, cap. vii., n. 59

[1] In nuptiis bona nuptialia diligantur proles, fides, sacramentum.—S. Aug., lib. i., *De myst. et concupisc.*, cap. xvi. n. 19.

Hujus procul dubio sacramenti res est ut mas et fœmina connubio copulati, quamdiu vivunt, inseparabiliter perseverent.—S. Aug., lib. i., *De nuptiis*, cap. x., n. 2.

[2] S. Aug., *De bono conjugali*, cap. xviii., n. 21.

[3] Council of Verona, 1181; II. Council of Lyons, 1374; Sacramentarians of St. Leon., 461; of St. Gelasius, 496; of St. Gregory the Great; Greek Sacramentarians; Liturgies of the Nestorians, Copts, Jacobites, Armenians.—(Cf. Perrone, *De matrimonio christiano*, tome i., cap. i., § i., art. 1.)

"If any one says that marriage is not truly and properly one of the seven sacraments of the Gospel Law, instituted by Christ Our Lord, but that it has been invented in the Church by men, and that it does not confer grace, let him be anathema."[1]

Observe, the council does not say there is a sacrament in marriage, but that marriage itself is a sacrament. These words are of sovereign importance. They protect the conjugal union against the usurpations of which we shall have to speak, and teach us that we may not separate these two things: the human act by which man and woman give themselves to each other, and the divine act by which grace is conferred. Like the religious and sacred character given to the conjugal tie by the mysterious power whose intervention in the natural marriage we have already stated, so also the sacrament arises from the contract. I say more: it is the contract itself, the contract invested by God with the power to produce grace in the same way as all outward signs which He, their supernatural author, has made the instruments of His almighty power. We cannot, then, say: here is the marriage, there the sacrament; the marriage contracted by the exchange of consent, the sacrament poured out like a beneficent oil on the contracted union. No. It is in the very exchange of consent that

---

[1] Si quis dixerit matrimonium non esse vere et proprie unum ex septem legis Evangelicæ sacramentum a Christo Domino institutum, sed ab hominibus in Ecclesia inventum; neque gratiam conferre, anathema sit.—Sess. 24, *De Matrimonio*, can. I.

the sacramental elements are found, from which there results not only a purely natural tie, as in primitive marriage, but also a supernatural tie, impregnated and penetrated with the grace of God.

Understand clearly this mystery, husbands who become by your union the stock of the Christian family, and recognize your dignity. You have received in baptism a participation in the priesthood of Jesus Christ, a character has been imprinted on your souls, sinking deeply into them as one makes deeper the canals through which shall pass the waters of a great river. This character gave you a right to the bounty and benefits of the divine life, and I have said it was a passive power, by which your regenerated souls became apt to receive sacred things. I ought to add to-day that for one circumstance in the Christian life there is in the baptismal character an active power which makes you resemble more closely the priesthood of Christ: it is the power of giving at the same time that you receive it the sacred thing which transforms marriage and makes it more holy than God made it at the beginning of the world.

When, standing in front of the altar and under the eyes of the Church, the young persons about to be united give their hands to each other, they are priests, priests like the sublime man whose greatness we lately celebrated, for, like him, they make and give a sacred thing. They say: Will you take me, I give myself.—It is the matter of the sacrament. They answer: I receive you for mine.—It is the form of the sacrament. And when the donation and acceptation are joined on both sides, the supernatural tie is made, grace bursts forth, the sacrament is perfected.

This sacrament does not pass away, says a learned theologian; it remains like the ineffable mystery which we adore on our altars and in our tabernacles. Just as the eucharistic species remain after the act which consecrates them, as the symbol of the spiritual food which they contain, so likewise the ordinary life of Christian husbands and wives, the outward manifestation of the tie which binds them, remains as the symbol of the indissoluble union between Christ and His Church, which it imitates.[1] This is why St. Paul calls marriage a great sacrament: *Sacramentum hoc magnum est.*

Further, gentlemen, this sacrament continues in the conjugal tie with all the virtuality which the exchange of oaths has given to it. It is not only before the altar that it produces grace, it retains the power of producing it in all circumstances and whenever the ordinary life of Christian husbands and wives requires it. And what grace! The holy Council of Trent has described it in a few words which leave nothing unsaid: "It is a grace

---

[1] Est matrimonium simile Eucharistiæ, quae non solum dum fit, sed etiam dum permanet, sacramentum est. Dum enim conjuges vivunt, semper eorum societas sacramentum est Christi et Ecclesiæ.... Nam negari non potest ipsos conjuges, simul cohabitantes, sive externam conjugum societatem et conjunctionem, esse materiale symbolum externum Christi et Ecclesiæ indissolubilem conjunctionem referens, quemadmodum in sacramento Eucharistiæ, consecratione peracta, remanent species consecratæ, quae sunt symbolum sensibile atque externum interni alimenti spiritualis.—Bellarmin, *De Matrimonio,* cap. vi.

which perfects natural love, strengthens the union into an absolute indissolubility, and sanctifies the persons married.[1]

Natural love allows itself to be captivated by those fragile charms which the cruel hand of time never spares. Every day this pitiless ravager of human beauty does its work. It fades the radiant color of youth, deforms the features, wrinkles the forehead, sprinkles the hair with its frost, bends the body, destroys, one after another, the attractions which speak to the eye, and at last there only remains before one a disfigured idol, which causes the foolishly captivated heart only regret of its fond adoration.

Natural love, however well founded on respect and esteem, does not always withstand the sudden revelations which place under our eyes the imperfections, faults, and vices of which we had not dreamt. Our shaken security, our menaced peace, discourage the poor heart, which believed itself so steadfast, and invite it to cease loving. Natural love, in a fallen creature, but little master of his passions, wearies of being attached to the same object. Inconstancy and caprice turn him, alas! too easily towards another, by whose side he forgets both his duty and his vows. Lamentable weakness, from which marriage has suffered in all ages!

---

[1] Gratiam vero, quæ naturalem illum amorem perficeret et indissolubilem unitatem confirmaret, conjugesque sanctificaret, ipse Christus, venerabilium sacramentorum institutor atque perfector, sua nobis passione promeruit.—Sess. 24, *De Matrimonio.*

But since it has been sanctified by Christ, grace perfects love. It renders it wise. It teaches it that nothing is perfect here below; that the infinite beauty of God is the only ideal capable of satisfying a heart eager for perfection; that when men have not all that they would wish, they must love what they have. It purifies the natural eye, renders uncomeliness bearable, infirmity touching, and old age and white hairs lovable.

Grace makes love patient. It strengthens it against the shock of known faults and against the too sudden revelation of those faults which have escaped its observation. Grace makes love just and merciful. It persuades it easily that, if we have to suffer, we make ourselves suffer, and that in married life more than elsewhere the evangelical maxim must be put into practice: "Bear ye one another's burdens." Instead of reproaches, it suggests excuses. It changes recrimination into good counsel, wise exhortation, gentle encouragement, amiable correction; it inclines the hearts, which it softens, to pardon easily. Finally, grace makes love faithful in duty; it makes it see in a bright daylight, which the clouds of fancy, caprice, misconception, and falsehood cannot darken, and makes it find in constancy an honor and joy for which it thanks God, He Who is so faithful even to those who injure Him.

True, gentlemen, this perfection of natural love by grace is already a strong guarantee of solidity for the conjugal tie, but the sacramental act contributes more to its support. It lays hold of it, transforms it, and so tightens the cords that they can be neither stretched nor broken. By rendering it more sacred through the permeation of His infinite virtue, God pledges Himself to show no more that indulgence for human weakness which obtained from Him formerly those permissions and dispensations which our perverse nature has so greatly abused.

Such is marriage. Twice honored by the intervention of God, at the solemn epochs of the creation and the redemption, it demands our respect, and I have the right to say to men: Touch it not, it is a holy thing. Yes, it is a holy thing. You must be deeply imbued with this truth, if you wish to agree with me in the conclusion which I shall draw from it. This conclusion can only confirm the words of St. Paul: This is a great sacrament: *Sacramentum hoc magnum est.*

Conference II.

The Conjugal Tie.

My Lord[1] and Gentlemen:—While it is required for a perfect marriage that the man and the woman inwardly consent to give themselves to each other, and that their consent be expressed by a verbal contract, yet the essence of marriage is not in the consent so expressed. Nor is it in the mutual giving and receiving of their persons. It is in the bond and the obligation which theologians call *conjunctio*,[2] and the Roman Catechism, the conjugal tie. That catechism is wholly impregnated with the spirit and doctrine of the holy Council of Trent, and from it I borrow the central idea from which proceed and around which gravitate the truths which I am about to explain.

The conjugal tie, made and knotted by the concurrence of two powers, the human will and the divine will, is the very essence of marriage. This tie, sacred in itself and made more sacred by the institution of the Sacrament of Matrimony, is a tie which cannot be divided, a bond that cannot be broken. It is one and indissoluble. These are the qualities of marriage which we must study.

There is no need, gentlemen, of asking your

---

[1] Monseigneur Richard, Archbishop of Paris.
[2] See Latin text in notes of preceding conference.

closest attention to this subject. You know well its importance at the present time, and you will, I hope, scrupulously attend to the development of these two propositions:—First, The indissoluble unity of the conjugal tie is a divine law. Second, That law is a law of progress and perfection in nature.

I.

God, Who is the principle of life, has diffused that principle throughout the world with boundless liberality, but He has not left it to itself. He has regulated the evolutions and determined the conditions of these prolific unions by which life is propagated. In this God is the absolute Master, and His will is the law of the beings whom He associates in His continued act of creation; but, gentlemen, when God had separated from every living thing the two privileged beings to whom He gave the empire of the world, and who were to be the stock of a race marked with the seal of the likeness of God, He willed that they should be indissolubly united to each other. If He did not express His will in words, as He did with regard to the tree of knowledge of good and evil, He spoke secretly of His design to the heart of the first man, and it was by a divine instinct, says the Church, that the father of humanity pronounced those celebrated words which I have lately quoted to you: " This is bone of my bones, and flesh of my flesh; she shall be called Woman, because she was taken out of man. Wherefore a man shall leave father and mother, and shall cleave to his wife; and they shall be two in one flesh."¹

You hear, gentlemen, two, and no more. And these two shall cleave to each other as the flesh and bone of Adam, from which the woman is formed, cleaved to his body: *Quamobrem adhærebit homo uxori suæ.* "Such is the will of God," says Tertullian, "manifested in this typical marriage, the form of which should be imitated by all men."² The law is not yet express and imperative, as it will become, but the generations which have issued from our first parents recognize its implicit authority, and for a long time the indissoluble unity of the conjugal tie is the rule of those who found families and multiply the human race.

Lamech, the first who violates it to satisfy his passion, is a man of blood and malediction.³ It is true that after the Deluge polygamy was established, and the law-giver of the Jewish people permitted, in certain cases, the rupture of the conjugal tie. God tolerated these practices, but the primitive institution of marriage still existed, awaiting better days. But during this expec-

---

¹ Matrimonii perpetuum indissolubilemque nexum primus humani generis parens divini Spiritus instinctu pronuntiavit cum dixit: *Hoc nunc os*, etc.—Conc. Trid., sess. 24, *Doctrina de Sacramento Matrimonii.*

² Et ideo homo Dei Adam et mulier Dei Eva, unis in terse nuptiis juncti formam hominibus Dei, de originis auctoritate, et prima Dei voluntate sanxerunt.—*De exhort. cast.*, cap. 5.

³ Numerus matrimonii a maledicto viro cœpit. Primus Lamech duabus maritatus, tres in unam carnem effecit.—Tertul., loc. cit.

Primus Lamech, sanguinarius et homicida, unam carnem in duas divisit uxores.—S. Hieron. lib. *Advers. Jovinianum.*

tation, God, the author of nature and the lawgiver of human life, has entire power to relax the obligations of a law to which He has not yet given its definite form. He knows better than any one else why He tolerates acts which His positive law and the first principles of natural law manifestly forbid. God may have permitted polygamy in order to hasten the multiplication of families and nations. He may have wished to reestablish a numerical equilibrium of the sexes, and spare His people the domestic crimes to which the impetuosity of their passions and their hardness of heart exposed them. It may have been His wish to allow the human family to experience the disorders of unbridled lust. We know not why He tolerated polygamy, but we do know that His tolerance does not excuse the license which passion takes against the wish of legitimate husband and wife, and for evil ends. It is only the arrogance which belongs to heresy that can accuse those of crime whom He has not condemned. The tolerance of God towards the generations of antiquity does not make Him forget His first design in the institution of marriage, and we may say of the indissoluble unity of the conjugal tie what St. Paul said of God Himself: *Non sine testimonio semetipsum reliquit*, "God left not Himself without testimony."[1] Just as in the midst of the darkness of idolatry the existence of the true God is attested by proofs so evident that the reason which does not submit to them is without excuse,

[1] Acts xiv. 16.

so also in the universal decay of marriage its unity and indissolubility are affirmed and declared by facts and by teaching which link the Christian restoration to the primitive institution. It is easy to guess from the language of Scripture to which side the law of nature and preference of God incline. The historical, lyrical, and prophetic books are full of precious indications in this respect. "We are the children of saints," says young Tobias to her whom he marries; "we must not be joined together like heathens that know not God.... Thou madest Adam of the slime of the earth, and gavest him Eve for a helper.... And now, Lord, Thou knowest that not for fleshly lust do I take my sister to wife, but only for the love of posterity, in which Thy name may be blessed forever and ever." And Sara completes this touching prayer: "Have mercy on us, O Lord, have mercy on us, and let us grow old both together in health."[1] She is the only woman and faithful spouse that Wisdom praises.

The Canticle of Canticles celebrates the mystical marriage which shall become the type of Christian marriage. Moses permitted the bill of divorce, but this act is surrounded by a crowd of legal precautions which can only be considered as so many

[1] Filii sanctorum sumus, et non possumus ita conjungi, sicut gentes quæ ignorant Deum..... Domine Deus patrum nostrorum, tu fecisti Adam de limo terræ, dedistique ei adjutorium Hevam. Et nunc, Domine, tu scis quia non luxuriæ causa accipio sororem meam conjugem, sed sola posteritatis dilectione, in qua benedicatur nomen tuum in sæcula sæculorum. Dixit quoque Sara: Miserere nobis, Domine, miserere nobis, et consenescamus ambo pariter sani.—Tob viii. 5-10.

protestations of the desire of God in opposition to its indulgence. It is a remarkable fact that those who profit by this indulgence, during the long period of time which elapses between the exodus and the captivity, are so few, and conceal themselves so well, that sacred history does not mention them. Among the nations where the word of God is never heard, some persistently marry but once; and barbarians even deserve this praise from a great historian: " Their virgins only marry one man, to make with him one body and one life. Their thought and desire do not reach beyond this, because it is their marriage that they love rather than a husband."[1] An old Indian legislator writes: "Man and woman make but one person. . . . . Woman is the companion of man in life, in death."[2] —In short, at the time when the kingly nation dishonored itself by the capricious and infamous divorces which demoralized Roman society, it did not expunge from its law this beautiful definition of marriage: *Divini humanique juris communicatio, consortium omnis vitæ, individuam vitæ consuetudinem retinens.*[3] "A common participation in the same law, divine and human; union for life in the same fate; the condition and habits of two lives which henceforth make but one."

In spite of these protestations, Roman relaxation

---

[1] Virgines accipiunt unum maritum, quomodo unum corpus, unamque vitam, nec ulla cogitatio ultra, nec longior cupiditas, ne tanquam maritum sed tanquam matrimonium ament.— Tacit., *De moribus Germanorum*, n. 19.

[2] Law of Manou.   [3] *Digest.*, xxiii.

triumphed, even to corruption. It would have triumphed in the long run over the indissoluble unity of the conjugal tie, if God, wearied with tolerance, had not solemnly restored that unity. He speaks no longer by the mouth of inspired men, but by the mouth of His Son. You have seen, gentlemen, this divine Bridegroom of our nature; you have heard Him when He enacted the institution of the sacrament. Hear Him again; for to-day it is His word that makes the law.

"And there came to Him the Pharisees tempting Him, and saying: Is it lawful for a man to put away his wife for every cause? Who answering, said to them: Have ye not read, that He Who made man from the beginning, made them male and female? And He said: For this cause shall a man leave father and mother, and shall cleave to his wife, and they two shall be in one flesh; therefore now they are not two, but one flesh. What therefore God hath joined together, let no man put asunder. They say to Him: Why, then, did Moses command to give a bill of divorce, and to put away? He said to them: Because Moses, by reason of the hardness of your heart, permitted you to put away your wives: but from the beginning it was not so. And I say to you, that whosoever shall put away his wife, except it be for fornication, and shall marry another, committeth adultery: and he that shall marry her that is put away, committeth adultery. His disciples say unto Him: If the case of a man with his wife be so, it is not expedient to marry. Who said to them: All men take not this word, but they to whom it is given."[1]

It is impossible, gentlemen, to teach more clearly that God, in the primitive institution of marriage, had in view the indissoluble unity of the conjugal tie; that this indissoluble unity is expressly desired and commanded by the New Law; that it permits no more exceptions; that tolerance is at an end; that dispensations are abolished forever. Those crimes even which may justify a separation do not break the tie which binds two lives to each other when they are married; the wife sent away from the conjugal roof on account of her unfaithfulness can only be replaced by adultery. This is hard for carnal man, but it is the law of the new world created by the Redeemer.

Such is the law. St. Paul promulgates it in the churches of Rome and of Corinth for the whole universe: " Know you not, brethren (for I speak to them that know the law), that the law hath dominion over a man, as long as it liveth? For the woman that hath a husband, whilst her husband liveth, is bound to the law: but if her husband be dead, she is loosed from the law of her husband. Therefore, whilst her husband liveth, she shall be called an adulteress if she be with another man: but if her husband be dead, she is delivered from the law of her husband: so that she is not an adulteress if she be with another man."[2] " But to them that are

---

[1] St. Matt. xix. 3-11.

[2] An ignoratis, fratres (scientibus enim legem loquor), quia lex in homine dominatur, quanto tempore vivit? Nam quæ sub viro est mulier, vivente viro, alligata est legi; si autem mortuus fuerit vir ejus, soluta est a lege viri. Igitur, vivente viro, vocabitur adultera si fuerit

married, not I, but the Lord commandeth, that the wife depart not from her husband: and if she depart, that she remain unmarried, or be reconciled to her husband. And let not the husband put away his wife."[1] In a word, the divine and inviolable law for husband and wife is to be bound by a tie which death alone can break.

It is the law. In the name of the indissoluble unity of the conjugal tie re-established by Christ, the successors of the apostles, the Fathers and the doctors of the Church, drive back before them the last resistance of Judaism and paganism, as well as the edicts and licenses of the princes of the earth. Monogamy, they say, has entered into Christian customs.[2] No more polygamy, Christ has abolished it.[3] One wife or none at all is the motto of the Christian.[4] As long as a man lives, no matter what may be his crimes, he remains the husband

---

cum alio viro; si autem mortuus fuerit vir ejus, liberata est a lege viri, ut non sit adultera si fuerit cum alio viro.—Rom. vii. 1-3.

[1] Iis autem, qui matrimonio juncti sunt præcipio, non ego, sed Dominus, uxorem a viro non discedere; quod si discesserit, manere innuptam, aut viro suo reconciliari, et vir uxorem non dimittat.—I. Cor. vii. 10-11.

[2] (Apud Christianos) temperantia adest, continentia exercetur, monogamia servatur, custoditur castitas Παρ' οἷς σωφροσύνη παρεστιν, ἐγκράτεια ἀσκεῖται, μονογαμία τηρεῖται, ἁγνεία φυλάσσεται.— Theophil. Antiochen., ad Antolycum, lib. iii. n. 25.

[3] Idem vir et Dominus (Christus) non amplius concedit polygamiam: Ἀλλ' ὁ αὐτὸς ἀνὴρ καὶ κύριος οὐ πολυγαμίαν ἔτι συγχωρεῖ. —Clemens. Alex., Strom., lib. iii., p. 461.

[4] Unius matrimonii vinculo libenter inhæremus. Cupiditatem procreandi, aut unam scimas, aut nullam.—Minucius Felix, in Octavio, n. 31.

of the wife whom he has married.¹ The sacrament thus ordains it.² Do not speak to us of the laws of divorce enacted by secular powers. Not these, but the laws which God has made shall judge us.³ The laws of Cæsar are one thing, the laws of Christ are another; what is permitted by Papinian is one thing, what is forbidden by the great St. Paul is another thing.⁴ Hear the law of God to which even those are subject who make laws: *Quæ Deus conjunxit homo non separet.*⁵

It is the law. The Roman Pontiffs with sovereign authority recall it to the memories of those two daring kings and people who try to escape it. It is the law. All the schools of theology proclaim and comment on it. In spite of the resistance of nature and of human power it is established

---

¹ Quamdiu vivit vir, licet adulter sit, licet sodomita, licet flagitiis omnibus coopertus, et ab uxore propter hæc scelera derelictus, maritus ejus reputatur, cui alterum virum accipere non licet.—S. Hieron. *Epist. ad Amandum.*

² Haud procul dubio sacramenti res est, ut mas et femina connubio copulati, quamdiu vivunt, inseparabiliter perseverent.—S. Aug. lib. i., *De Nuptiis*, cap. x.

³ Ne mihi leges ab exteris conditas legas, præcipientes dari libellum repudii, et divelli. Neque enim juxta illas judicaturus est te Deus in die illa, sed secundum eas quæ ipse statuit: Μὴ γάρ μοι τοὺς παρὰ τοῖς ἔξωθεν κειμένους νόμους ἀναγνῶς, τοὺς κελεύοντας διδόναι βιβλίον ἀποστασίου, καὶ ἀρίστασθαι. Οὐ γὰρ δὴ κατὰ τούτους σοι μέλλει κρίνειν τοὺς νόμους ὁ Θεὸς ἐν τῇ ἡμέρᾳ ἐκείνῃ, ἀλλὰ καθ' οὓς αὐτὸς ἔθηκε.—S. Chrysost., Homil. ii., *De Matrimonio.*

⁴ Aliæ sunt leges Cæsarum, aliæ Christi; aliud Papinianus, aliud Paulus noster præcipit.—S. Hieron., *Epist. ad Oceanum*, n. 3.

⁵ Audi legem Domini, cui obsequantur etiam qui leges ferunt; quæ Deus, etc.—S. Ambros., in cap. vi. Luc., n. 5.

wherever churches are founded. Fifteen centuries old, it reigns uncontested at the period when Luther inaugurates the age of moral decay which tends to bring the world regenerated by Christ back to the loose and corrupt manners of antiquity. Luther, this libertine monk, restless under the yoke of religion, aspires to release himself from the vows which bind him to perpetual chastity. As an apology for the scandal which he is giving to the Christian world he finds nothing better than to deny the qualities of unity and indissolubility which were restored to marriage by Christ. And as if the liberty of divorce were not sufficient to gain for him the favor of the dissolute princes whose protection he covets, he allows them to practise polygamy.

Polygamy, says he, is after all but a return to patriarchal customs.[1] But this return must be discreet, so as not to affright the people accustomed by the Christian law to conjugal unity. Luther is ashamed of the license which he grants, but the watchful Church sees in it an open door by which corruption of manners is about to enter into the Christian family. It is time to determine the dogmatic formula of the law and to place it under the protection of anathema. Anathema, then, says the Council of Trent to those who permit Christians to have many wives, as if it were not forbidden by any divine law.[2] Anathema to those

[1] Profitebatur Lutherus se "poligamiæ consuetudinem nec introducere velle, nec improbare, posse autem quia Patrum exempla adhuc libera sunt."—*Comment.* in cap. xvi. Genes. Cit. Bellarm.

[2] Si quis dixerit licere christianis plures simul habere uxores, et hoc nulla lege divina esse prohibitum, anathema sit.—Sess. xxiv. can. 2.

who pretend that the conjugal tie can be broken.¹ Anathema to those who accuse of error the infallible authority of the Church when she affirms that not even adultery has power to dissolve the union which God has made.²

This is the law, gentlemen. Its origin is not doubtful. God Himself proclaimed it implicitly and prophetically in the beginning of time, and explicitly and definitely at the solemn epoch when the world was redeemed. When the Creator brought the world out of nothing and filled it with life, He gave to that life, with the power of multiplying itself, the rules and laws of its prolificness. Jesus Christ, the Creator of a moral and religious world, exercised the same power. He gave it a new life, and He certainly had the right to regulate the conditions of the unions from which a holy race was to be born. Christ does nothing extraordinary. He connects the regeneration of humanity with the immaculate creation, passing over all the ages that sin had dishonored. He determines, He limits, He fixes by an absolute law the divine plan which the human race would have originally fol-

---

[1] Si quis dixerit propter hæresim, aut molestam cohabitationem, aut affectatam absentiam a conjuge, dissolvi posse matrimonii vinculum, anathema sit.—Ibid., can. 5.

[2] Si quis dixerit Ecclesiam errare, cum docuit et docet, juxta evangelicam et apostolicam doctrinam, propter adulterium alterius conjugum matrimonii vinculum non posse dissolvi; et utrumque, etiam innocentem, qui causam adulterio non dedit, non posse, altero conjuge vivente, aliud matrimonium contrahere; mœcharique eum, qui dimissa adultera, aliam duxerit, et eam, quæ, dimisso adultero, alii nupserit; anathema sit.—Ibid., can. 7.

lowed, without hindrance or contradiction, had it preserved its original innocence. It was His right as Creator to do so.

It was also Christ's right as Redeemer. In order to redeem the world He had humiliated the divine majesty by uniting it with our fallen nature. That union was full of suffering, and should be a source of life and glory for us. Was it not right that the Redeemer should make the human family submit to the unity and indissolubility of marriage as a small return for the fruitful humiliations of His Incarnation?

In establishing the unity and indissolubility of marriage Jesus Christ merely exercises His right as Benefactor. In redeeming man, Christ transforms him. He puts grace in all the phases of his spiritual life. It is grace which begets him supernaturally, grace which increases and strengthens him, grace which nourishes and restores him, grace which cures him of his faults, and reconciles him to God; it is grace which perfects his purification, and opens to him the gates of eternity; grace which gives him dignity and divine powers in the priesthood; grace which unites him to her whom he has chosen for the companion of his life.

In sanctifying the marriage union, has not Christ the right to show Himself exacting? And if the indissoluble unity of the conjugal tie demands from husband and wife both effort and sacrifice, can they complain without ingratitude, since the sacrament which ennobles their yoke gives them the courage and strength to bear the sacred burden until death, if they receive it with pure hearts?

Finally, gentlemen, the legislation of the conjugal tie is the right of Christ in His office as our Great Exemplar. Man is the image and likeness of God; the Christian is the image and likeness of Christ. He should be so in everything. As an indissoluble unity in perfect love is the condition of the marriage between Christ and His Church, so also is the marriage of the Christian with her whom he marries, in order that, on one side as on the other, we may say, in the words of the Apostle, "This is a great mystery:" *Mysterium hoc magnum est.*

Yes, gentlemen, a great mystery. And in the shadows of this great mystery your Christian souls should submit to the certain law of God, even if you should find in the world of nature no aspiration, no law which justifies its holy austerity. But it is not so. Nature gives to the law of indissoluble union its full approval, for it is a law of progress and perfection.

II.

Let us first understand clearly, gentlemen, the meaning of this word—Nature. The great majority of those who rebel against the indissoluble unity of the conjugal tie do not attach the same meaning to it as we do. For them, nature does not go beyond the gloomy and excitable region of the appetites, and definitely, it is the human beast which concerns them more than anything else in the question of marriage. All that prevents the gratification of the animal man, all that condemns him to obey a nobler power, is regarded with abhorrence by their materialistic philosophy. To oppose the beast, is to oppose nature.

We do not thus understand the word, gentlemen. For us, nature is the whole man: the carnal man with his appetites and his power of generation; the spiritual man, with his reason, heart, free activity, knowledge of duty, and capacity for virtue. This man God had created perfect and master of the world. Was it not right that, in order to obey the divine command which desired his reproduction, he should be distinguished from all other creatures by the most perfect of unions? What is this union, gentlemen? Let us seek in the creation.

We look for it in vain where promiscuousness or polygamy are practised. But beyond the regions purely animal we find it at the head of all unions. It is the union of one with one alone and forever. It is monogamy, the true marriage, the perfect state, in which are realized all the conditions of intimacy and stability indicated by the word *union* in the highest and fullest sense of the word.

It is evident, gentlemen, to any one who has an idea of order, of progress, of perfection, that God responded to a desire of nature and to a call of the royal prerogatives of man, when He imposed on our first parents the law of the indissolubility of the conjugal tie, and made the multiplication of the most perfect of living beings dependent on a most perfect union.

It is also evident that man fell from the height where he governed nature when he began to imitate in marriage the unions of inferior beings; and it is evident that Christ led humanity back into a path of progress and perfection when He restored the primitive institution of marriage, and explicitly and definitely promulgated the law of its indissoluble unity.

Let us enter into human life itself and there apply the law of Christian marriage. You will see that I have spoken well in calling it a law of progress and perfection. It is indeed the law which belongs to true love; it is a school of virtue, the cement of the family, and the honor of human society. We cannot fully explain the entirety of the gift which two human beings make to each other of their persons, without seeking its cause in that deep and powerful sentiment which makes the heart beat, and which we call love. I do not blush to speak of it, for, if men have soiled it, God has purified it. It was noble and great in the young heart of our first father, when he called to his arms the bone of his bones and the flesh of his flesh; it can be noble and great in the hearts of those who, like our first parents, marry under the eye of God. Do not seek this love in the feverish passion whose throbs are evoked by carnal beauty, a passion strong as a tempest and as fleeting, too strained not to weary the soul, too attached to perishable attractions not to perish with them. True love knows how to free itself from the senses and to lay hold of that immaterial beauty on which time and the forces of nature have no power. It does not allow itself to be ensnared, but chooses its object; and the choice made, it says to itself: "Here is my rest forever," *Hæc requies in sæculum sæculi.* It is union that it desires, union that it seeks; an intimate, profound, complete union, so energetically expressed in these words of the Sacred Scriptures: "Two in one flesh," *Duo in carne una.* The more extended its rights, the better it understands its duties; and if it expects that they shall be given to it in all sincerity and without reserve, it gives itself with the same plenitude. By dividing his heart, a man who truly loves would consider himself debased; he would accuse himself of falsehood had he a thought of taking back what he has given; and he only fully and willingly expresses himself when he can say: "I am yours as you are mine, I am yours entirely and forever. Our lives henceforth are but one from now until death. 'Favor is deceitful and beauty is vain.'[1] But if favor and beauty have been allurements for me, there are other riches which I covet, which I pursue, which I esteem and love. On the ruins of those charms which allure and speak to the senses, these possessions appear to me more beautiful, more desirable, more worthy of attachment. Let us leave behind that which is perishable and let us love each other always!"

Is it not thus, gentlemen, that you understand and feel real love? Is it not thus that noble hearts understand and feel it? Is it not unnecessary to

---

[1] Prov. xxxi. 30.

seek far for the law which is suitable for it in conjugal union? It spontaneously precedes it, it is the law of indissoluble union.

I say in the second place, gentlemen, that the indissoluble unity of the conjugal tie is a school of virtue. However pure and strong true love may be, it needs to be protected by the law of duty, and to be strengthened by the practice of virtue, the most beautiful ornament of human dignity.

There is one virtue which indissolubility of marriage imposes on true love at its first approach. It is prudence. We do not bind ourselves forever without weighing the chains which we wish to carry; we do not give ourselves entirely and forever without sounding the abyss whither we are going to plunge. The blind passion of the senses is capable of this folly, but true love does not bind itself or give its confidence except in good earnest. Warned by the law which shall bind it, it waits, gets information, seeks under outward attractions and advantages those amiable and solid qualities which may assure it peace and happiness. It asks of the present favorable auguries for the future. It is possible that true love may be deceived, and then other virtues can repair its error, but without doubt it most frequently owes to the austere law which has made it prudent the tranquillity and joy of the hearth where its life is mingled with another life.

The indissoluble unity of marriage is more than a school of prudence. It is a school of justice. Justice is more or less outraged where the conjugal tie is divided and broken. It is generally the wife who suffers from the outrage. The competition of our loves diminishes her share, and she becomes the humiliated slave of a capricious passion. The wife brings into the common life the charms of her sex and the inestimable treasure of her modesty. Who shall give her back her charms if the husband has the power to put her away when he grows tired of her faded beauty and withered flesh? He would keep all his advantages, and she would lose her best treasures! If the husband has that power, then God lied when, on the day He completed the work of His creation, He said: "Let us make him a help like unto himself:" *Faciamus ei adjutorium simile sibi.* If the husband can sever the marriage tie we must believe that woman brought only an inferiority of right and an inferiority of nature into the first marriage union, so mysteriously prepared and so solemnly blessed to serve as a type of all future marriages. Such was not the case, gentlemen. In the design of God woman was the normal complement of man, and the tie which unites them must be knotted by justice.

It is indissoluble unity which brings into marriage this holy justice, suppressing all rivalry of love and assuring an equality of gifts as well as their continuance through life to both; the husband belonging solely, entirely, and forever to his wife, and the wife, solely, entirely, and forever to her husband.

But the perpetual double life cannot be to-day

what it might have been if humanity had preserved the privileges of its innocence. Between two fallen and fatally imperfect natures it is impossible that there should not be unexpected revelations and sad shocks in which souls are wounded. And if wills were free to retract, they might take counsel only of bad temper and human weakness to break a union become hard and heavy to bear. But the law of indissolubility restrains and obliges them to practise a virtue in which the greatness of man is revealed. That virtue is fortitude. Fortitude, which combats the defects and faults incidental to married life, and strives to lessen, if it cannot remove them; fortitude, which bears with patience the sad shocks it is impossible to avoid, and resists the impulses which test the strength of the indestructible marriage tie; fortitude, which knows how to subdue pride and ask for pardon. This virtue of fortitude is permeated with the unction of a charity that is rich in forethought, in pity, and in the loving exchange of sacrifice.

This is not all. Ancient philosophy invited men to moral progress and to perfection by the noble maxim, "Bear and forbear:"—*sustine, abstine*. The law of the unity and indissolubility of the marriage tie applies that maxim with sovereign authority to married life. The fortitude which bears with the trials of conjugal life should be completed by the temperance which abstains. One of the ends of marriage is to calm the turbulence of the flesh, but there are occasions when it does not attain that end. Those who know not how to resist the animal promptings of man demand other unions; but the man who is regenerated by Christ and is obedient to His law knows that the senses have no rights opposed to duty. He knows, too, that it is good and even necessary that the soul should from time to time assert her dignity, and should exercise her dominion over the lower promptings of the senses by keeping from them the pleasures they covet. When the senses are disciplined by temperance, they leave the field open to the pleasures of the heart, the noblest and sweetest that man can taste.

You have often heard it said, gentlemen, that we must make a virtue of necessity. Nowhere is that old proverb better applied than to the indissoluble unity of the conjugal tie. If the divine law does violence to our animal inclinations, it is so far in perfect accord with reason, which wishes the progress and perfection of our moral life.

God has not forged the indestructible chain of marriage for the mere purpose of satisfying the wishes of true love and opening for husbands and wives a school of great virtue. He has had care of a feeble and charming being, who will need for some time the double protection of strength and tenderness. Admirable arrangement of Providence! The more perfect the union of life with life, the slower the growth of its offspring. The being born from the fortuitous and blind meetings of promiscuousness finds at its birth the elements necessary for its development, and it has organs which act without delay in appropriating and assimilating them. If a more perfect instinct brings the sexes together, life needs for some time the assistance of the beings that gave it existence. But it is only for a season. The animal soon learns all that is necessary to take care of itself. It is altogether different where love enlightened by reason makes its choice. It is the privilege of the human being that the child demands for many years the solicitude and care of its parents to succor its helplessness. How powerful and tenacious are the ties between parents and child! It is truly said of the father and mother "they are two in one flesh:" *duo in carne una.* They are one by the blood of their veins, by the love of their hearts, in that flesh taken from their own flesh which reproduces their features and bears the impression of their souls. They are one in that fragile flesh whose life will be extinguished if not sustained and guarded with affectionate and untiring care; in that mysterious flesh in which the dormant soul awaits its awakening to thought and will.

"Marriage," says an eloquent bishop, "creates between parents and children strong and indissoluble ties, and yet some would wish it to be in itself only a fragile tie! But then the effects would be greater than their cause."[1] Father, mother, should you shut your ears to the voice of God,

---

[1] Il matrimonio crea vincoli indissolubili tra i coniugi ed i figli; e sarebbe esso un vincolo solubile; sarebbe mai, che gli effetti fossero maggiori della loro causa.—Mgr. Bonomelli, bishop of Cremona, Pastoral Instruction: *Sul Divorzio.*

you can never stifle the voice of nature which bids you remain united. Remain united each to each. Another love would turn you away from your duty and awaken jealous and quarrelsome passions which would disturb the peace of your hearth.[1] Remain united! father, to protect the wife who devotes herself day and night to the little creature to whom you have given life; mother, to accomplish without uneasiness and without fear your noble task of devotion.[2] Remain united! in order that the light of your reason and the tenderness of your hearts may penetrate the soul of your child. Remain united! to cast into this virgin soil the seed of those virtues without which man has no right to live; remain united! to cultivate together the sacred germs which you have sown. There must be two persons to cause the dawn of life, two to guide it to its complete development. A father alone is authority too severe, reason too cold, strength to weighty; a mother all alone is love without restraint, gentleness without guidance, tenderness without correction. Both are needful for education. Nature has joined and mingled them together as two elements which complete

---

[1] Non facile potest esse pax in familia ubi uno viro plures uxores junguntur, cum non possit unus vir sufficere ad satisfaciendum pluribus uxoribus ad votum; et etiam quia communicatio plurium in uno officio causat litem.—*Summ. Theol.*, supp., quæst. 45, a. 1.

[2] Matrimonium ex intentione naturæ ordinatur ad educationem prolis, non solum ad aliquod tempus, sed per totam vitam prolis. Ideo cum proles sit commune bonum viri et uxoris, oportet societatem eorum perpetuo permanere indivisam, secundum legis naturæ dictamen.—Ibid, quæst. 47, a. 1.

each other, and whence light and heat spring forth in the soul of the child.[1]

Fathers, mothers, remain, then, united, in order to multiply life around you, and to surround yourselves with a crown of living beings who shall be your glory, because they will reproduce your virtues. Remain united! that your children may return to you, in tender respect and pious help, all the good you shall have done them. Remain united! that you may see yourselves live again in the offspring of those who are the issue of your generous life. Remain united! to serve as a pattern to those who shall become united after you, and to cement by your unchangeable fidelity the sacred unity of the family.

Glorious are those families where the indissoluble unity of the conjugal tie links the past with the future, and creates those peaceful traditions through which each generation seeks its ancestors! In them are never heard the groans of love betrayed, or complaints of desertion. In them are not found children hatefully disposed, to whom has been transferred the sad heritage of a father's angry passions or a mother's feelings of

[1] Abbandonate la tutta (l'educazione) al solo padre: voi generalmente avrete l'autorità che riesce dura, l'intelligenza che e fredda e la forza che aggrava; lasciate la in balla della sola madre, e avrete l'amore senza autorita, la dolcezza e la tenerezza senza il correttivo dell' intelligenza e della forza. La natura stessa pertanto vuole accoppiati e fusi insieme i due elementi necessarii alla educazione dei figli; l'elemento paterno e l'elemento materno: sono due forze, che per produrre il loro effetto, vogliono essere unite; sono duo raggi, che si debbono concentrare sopra di uno punto per ottenerne la luce ed il calore.—Mgr. Bonomelli, *Sul Divorzio*.

rancor. In them gloomy jealousy is not suffered, nor the deep antagonism caused by divided love and the injustice of capricious repudiation. Glorious families! They are respected, and their alliance is sought, and by their alliances they cause to radiate around them the honesty, peace, and prosperity of which they are the centres. Glorious families! a perpetual honor to society, wherein they are the elements of a unity indispensable to every people that desires to live.

I say no more to-day, gentlemen. The truths you have just heard will be more fully developed when, in the next conference, we shall speak of what is opposed to them. For the moment I think I have attained my end, which was to prove that nature fully acquiesces in the divine law of the indissoluble unity of the conjugal tie. This law ennobles love, ennobles the moral life, ennobles the family, ennobles society; it is, therefore, a law of progress and perfection.

We hear certain reformers of conjugal society say that they willingly dispense with that perfection, and taking the world as it is, they are content to chastise its vices. Miserable failure of Protestant cowardice opposing the sublime character which Christ by His law has imprinted on married life. Who has the right to oppose nature when God pleases to help it become perfect? Who has the right to make humanity go backward when God urges it forward? Contemptible reformers, you make liars of yourselves, for you are always boasting that you are men of progress. You, men of progress! and you mock a law which gives true love its rights, places man in the happy necessity of perfecting his moral life, consolidates the family, and assures to society the elements of a glorious existence. You, men of progress! and you would bring us back to the time when fallen man degraded marriage and lived like a beast. You, men of progress! and you oppose the divine impulse which tends to raise the married man above his animal nature, and to place him on the royal summit from which he is lord of all nature.

False reformers, be silent rather than speak falsehood! The men of progress are the apostles and faithful observers of the indissoluble unity of the conjugal tie. Christ has made them see depraved humanity reduced to the level of the beast through its faithlessness to the primitive institution of marriage, and He has said to them: "Go up higher:" *Ascende superius.* And they, obeying at the same time the noble aspirations of nature and the voice of God, have nobly answered: "Let us ascend:" *Ascendamus.*

Conference III.

Divorce.

My Lord[1] and Gentlemen:—In our last conference I promised to give counter-proofs of the truths explained in it, and I shall do so now.

As we have already said, the properties of the conjugal tie are its unity and indissolubility. These properties, strengthened by a divine law and by the grace of the sacrament, answer the requirements of nature, which demands for man and wife the most perfect union, and which also aspires to progress and perfection in the individual, in the family, and in society. Your noble souls, I am persuaded, are in full sympathy with this doctrine: still I deem it my duty to show you the worthlessness of the arguments of the so-called reformers who would change the character of the conjugal tie.

We can say this much to the credit of the opponents of the divine law: They do not want to revive the manners of ancient times, the free practice of which Luther permitted to people of rank. We can also say that they agree with us about the eminently progressive character of monogamy, and the disadvantages and inconveniences of polygamy.

[1] Monseigneur Richard, Archbishop of Paris.

In polygamy man abandons himself to the agitating pleasures of sensation, to the ruin of his intellectual and moral life, and to the degradation of his dignity; in it the degraded wife becomes the servant—one might say the slave—of a base passion, and the human family is like a flock divided and troubled by jealousies and quarrels. In a word, polygamy brings the human being to the level of the beast. Eighteen centuries of Christianity have made polygamy so rare and odious that the bitterest enemies of the Christian law of marriage look with contempt and disgust on the harems of the East and the licentious follies of Mormonism. But it is different when there is question of the indissoluble unity of the marriage tie. There is quite a number of meddlers in philosophy and law who look upon the indissolubility of the conjugal tie as a tyrannical law. They think that modern society should have the right to break a yoke which human nature is unable to bear.

Let us first examine, gentlemen, the arguments brought against the divine law. I hope to show you how worthless they are.

I shall then show you that divorce, by which it is proposed to replace the divine law, is worse than all the evils for which indissolubility is held responsible, and that it is a principle of decay for human society.

I.

When special decrees are made for individuals they are proportioned to their strength. Laws have not this narrow character. They look to the general well-being, and are made for the multitude. If by their application to individuals they may be inconvenient, and impose here and there a greater restraint, that is no reason for their abrogation when they are conducting human society forward in the path of progress and perfection.

Such is the law of indissolubility. It is a law for a race, ordained, as you have seen, for the perfection of our nature and for the general well-being of humanity. That the individual should sometimes suffer from it, is not astonishing; to adduce this suffering as a pretext to get rid of the law is absurd. Admit in principle that a law can and should be suppressed because it bears hardly in some of its special applications, and you will render all order and morality impossible.

It is, however, in some such fashion that the opponents of the indissolubility of the marriage tie proceed. They tell in bitter language some of the inconveniences of the divine law, and even invent others to enlarge the sum of their grievances. You might make a volume of the reasons for not accepting the law of indissolubility which they accumulate against it. I will not enter in detail on these inconveniences, griefs, and reasons for non-acceptance of the divine law. To deal justly, it will suffice to reduce them to the three following heads:

First, the law of indissoluble unity is an outrage on human liberty, which it binds with the chains of slavery;

Secondly, the law of indissoluble unity tends to frustrate the principal intention of marriage;

Thirdly, the law of indissoluble unity exposes those whom it irrevocably unites to being deprived unjustly and hopelessly of the happiness to which they are entitled when they enter into conjugal society; it exasperates and urges them to crime.

Liberty is so great a possession that we must never give it up except in good earnest, and never abdicate our right to take it again. To bind one's self forever, as is done in an indissoluble marriage; to forge, in a moment, a chain which can never be broken, this is criminal folly. Are we master of the heart which says to us to-day: "I love you"? Are we sure of our own hearts? Can we foresee the shortcomings of weakness and the betrayals of inconstancy? Is it allowable to throw one's self body and soul into the future, as if one were sure of meeting with no deceptions? Rash young people, who exchange eternal promises, you will some day regret the heavy and insupportable chain which you have foolishly riveted around your liberty, and you will be condemned to the inevitable shame of either breaking your word or submitting yourselves to an irremediable slavery.

You will lament your misfortune. You will blame yourselves for your fault. Tears and reproaches, all will be useless. No, no, you cannot, you should not expose yourselves to these humiliations and misfortunes. Become united, if you love each other, but keep your liberty as a guarantee against the surprises of the future. And if there is a law which demands this sacrifice from you, reply to it with all the strength of your outraged dignity:—*Non licet!* It is not lawful.

Gentlemen, I agree with the apologists of liberty on this point: that liberty is a great possession, and that it is a criminal folly to give it up forever without forethought for the future and without provision for the consequences of this delicate and terrible sacrifice. But listen: If liberty is a possession, it belongs to me. I am its master and can dispose of it as I will, to-day, to-morrow, in the future, forever, provided I dispose of it wisely and usefully. I know what is meant by indissoluble union; I have contracted one with the holy religion of which I wear the habit; and in spite of the disappointments and sorrows I may have found in it, and which I had foreseen, I do not at all regret the sacrifice I made to it of my liberty, for it has been repaid with inestimable goods.

It is the good in a work that we ought to look at, and when this good deserves a great sacrifice, we should make it. Now, gentlemen, you know the good of the conjugal union strengthened by indissolubility: it ennobles love, it ennobles the moral life, it ennobles the family, it ennobles society. For this it is well worth while to bind yourselves forever. The man who is timid and selfishly careful of his well-being will only take account of the evils possible in the future in a life united with another life; the generous and wise man takes into account the certain benefits, the noble sincerity and constancy which true love should experience in becoming united to another love; the sacred equality of gifts commanded by justice; the immense advantages which result from the persevering union of two hearts and two lives for the education of children, the strengthening and uniting of the family; the honor that all society receives by incorporating into it those elements of stability supplied by families where traditions unite the past with the future, where the indissoluble unity of the conjugal tie causes peace and honesty to flourish. The wise man is not blind to the adverse chances which may cause him to regret having bound himself. As far as is possible for human prudence, he prepares against them. But his precautions taken, he places above the evils he may fear the great good he hopes and desires to obtain, and even if he has to struggle and suffer, he binds himself forever. Let it not be said that this is not permitted. Then all noble enterprises to which generous and bold souls unite their lives would be condemned. I maintain that it is a most beautiful and praiseworthy act of liberty to bind one's self forever to a good which benefits the whole world.

To be bound in that way, gentlemen, is not to be a slave. Indissolubility is not intended to weigh as a dishonorable yoke, but to direct and lead on the road of moral progress that liberty which she binds. By making itself respected, indissolubility imposes upon a man courageous efforts, which restrain his passions, correct his vices, lessen his faults, perfect his good qualities, strengthen his virtues, and multiply his good actions. Man does not lower and degrade himself by submitting to and obeying the divine law of the indissoluble unity of the marriage tie, but by revolting against it.

Besides, the opponents of indissolubility have no right to show themselves so delicate and modest with regard to the pretended outrage done to liberty by the perpetual engagement which binds the two lives of those who marry each to the other. There are among them a great number to whom we might retort the reproach of criminal folly which they make against us. In attacking the indissolubility of marriage they attack religion and hope to wound it mortally. But in this they only obey the word of command given by the pitiless sects of which they are the sworn slaves. They themselves are tied by the sinister promises which have bound them in a dark conspiracy of evil against all that is holy and just. If they wished to break their chains, could they do it with impunity? No. The secret marriages of perverse souls are too surely sealed for a divorce to be permitted them. And it is these slaves of iniquity who reproach most bitterly honest and Christian souls for the eternal oaths by which they bind themselves to obtain the greater good from conjugal society, at the risk of suffering. Let them wash away the opprobrium which binds their liberty before concerning themselves with ours. We do not accept either their advice or their censure; for honest men and Christians only sacrifice for good reasons the liberty they have a right to dispose of for well doing; it is liberty itself which accomplishes this sacrifice, and it is one of her noblest actions.

Granted, will some one say to me. Let liberty bind itself. But still it ought to be sure of attaining the end it has in view when so doing. Among the benefits by which marriage is honored, theology, agreeing with the instincts of nature, places children in the first rank : *Primum bonum matrimonii est proles.* It is in order to see themselves live again in these charming beings that man and woman exchange their oaths of love. The child is their honor, for in him they participate in the paternity of God ; the child is their happiness, for in him their hearts meet to love each other still more. Happy the homes where the husband, regarding with a tender eye the dear offspring of his life, can say : " I shall not die entirely ! " *Non omnis moriar !* Happy the homes where conjugal love reposes and refreshes itself in another holy and legitimate love.

But alas! there are homes not blessed with the presence of children, where the husband and wife, in sad tête à tête, await in vain the offspring they desire and which should rejoice their lives. If only they might leave each other, and seek elsewhere a fertile union. But no ; indissolubility rivets them to perpetual sterility, interminably prolongs their disappointment, and in their persons outrages marriage itself in depriving it hopelessly of its chief benefit. Have we not reason to revolt against such a law ?

Yes, gentlemen, the opponents of indissolubility would have a right to revolt if sterility in marriage were the rule, and fecundity the exception. But you are aware that it is precisely the contrary. We should return here to the principle which served us as a starting-point; namely, that in the general application of a law individuals may suffer, but that that is not a sufficient reason for abrogating the law. From the lowest depth to the summit of living nature, everywhere the great law of reproduction suffers from exceptions. In blessing the germs with which fertile virtue should people the universe, God did not bind Himself to guarantee them from all the accidents which might limit their power. How many lives are lost in this way in the immense germination of life which takes place every day! If you ask me, Why? I reply, It is a secret of the providence of God. Those who believe in Providence should adore its decrees and leave its laws to fulfil themselves. As to the law with which we are now concerned, no one can assure us that the rupture of the conjugal tie would always remedy sterile unions; everybody knows that, if left to himself, man is capable of criminal fraud in order to free himself from a salutary and beneficent yoke as soon as he finds it too hard to bear.

Besides, for husbands and wives who know how to submit to the holy will of God their united life is not without its compensations. They have not to dread those domestic catastrophes which desolate the hearth, nor the terrible blows which bruise the hearts of parents when they lose by death the dear little ones in whom they had placed all their affections and hopes; not having to diffuse their love over other lives, they become more attached to the one which is united to them. They love each other so much the more as they feel themselves necessary to one another. If their love needs other effusion than in their intimate union, they know how to make for themselves a family of those who shall benefit by their deeds of charity.

I heard it said one day of a noble and virtuous couple, to whom God had denied the happiness of a family:—" What a misfortune they have no children!" An old priest who knew them replied: "They have no children! Go and say that to the unfortunate creatures whom they help, to the afflicted whom they console, to the poor little ones who owe to them their daily bread, clothing, instruction, and what is better still, the principles of faith and the holy love of God. Do not pity them, for they are happy: happy in emulating each other in good works, happy in relating in private their deeds of charity, happy in hearing around them the blessings of the unfortunate, blessings which shall follow them to the place of their eternal rest. In this blessed home there is a great privation, but no misfortune."

But the opponents of the indissolubility of the marriage tie will say: Granted, but still it is needful that souls should understand one another, that lives should be blended, and that all the benefits summed up by your theologians in this one word, *fides*, that is to say, harmony of disposition, gentle forethought, loving support, mutual confidence, inviolable fidelity, should be the reward of an eternal engagement. To count upon it, is to illy understand the caprices, the weaknesses, and, let us say it frankly, the perverse inclinations of human nature. If there are people happy together, let them remain united, we have no intention of disturbing their happiness. But for a few well assorted couples, how many unsuitable ones are there, whose conjugal happiness has lasted no longer than the time of their honey-moon; and this honey-moon has been succeeded by a period of bitter regret.

It is impossible to describe the innumerable evils that afflict the home where man and wife are bound together forever; there is no end to them. Here, it is the unexpected revelation of repugnant infirmity or of dishonor that has been kept secret; there, the sudden explosion of passions and vices hitherto cleverly restrained; here, faults which bristle up at the least contradiction and discourage the most enduring patience; there, degrading habits which cannot be concealed, and sometimes public infamy which the law chastises; here, venomous hatred incessantly plotting; there, rage which bursts forth like thunder; here, insults, threats, quarrels, brutality, violence; there, abominable perfidy; here, infidelity enveloped in cunning and falsehood; there, treasonable love insolently installed at the domestic hearth. All, in short, that can divide spirits, rend and make hearts desperate, and kill love forever. Is not this what is found in a number of households? And in these prisons of moral misery and crime you would keep a man and wife chained to each other like two convicts bearing the same burden? Both guilty, sometimes, because they have only met with deception each in the other, and oftener the innocent is chained to the guilty. But this is as absurd as it is odious. Does not reason itself say, set these miserable creatures at liberty instead of prolonging their torture; break the barbarous tie of indissolubility which condemns them to a perpetual privation of the happiness they had dreamed of, and which they had a right to expect when they entered into conjugal society. If you hold them bound, you are responsible for the passions which swell in the depths of their exasperated souls, and which give utterance to the ferocious cry:—kill him, kill her!

This is, gentlemen, the hardest blow of the opponents of the divine law. I am not affected by it, and I still preserve sufficient presence of mind to remark to my opponents that they abuse the use of sombre tints, and that to generalize and exaggerate evil in order that it may serve as an argument, is more clever than manly. Statistics do not portray marriage in such black colors in those countries where the indissolubility of the conjugal tie is still religiously respected. I do not deny the imperfections of poor human nature. When these imperfections marry, it is not astonishing that they vex one another, and that those who have united them experience some inconveniences, but this does not lead regularly to catastrophe or even to unhappiness.

Most marriages resemble those temperate regions where the barometer oscillates between storm and settled fine weather. These oscillations may be disagreeable, but not so disagreeable as to make us wish to leave our happy climates, and to take refuge at the poles, the tropics, or the equator. Strained and violent conditions in marriage are the exception, and it is not the law which is responsible for them, but those who criminally or imprudently create them. An author too fond of these paradoxical theses, and who has made for himself a name in the question of divorce, has lately written thus: " There is generally but little pity for the griefs and misadventures of a married man, because they are only the disappointments he might easily have foreseen. All misfortunes are more or less voluntary ones. One has desired to be more happy than he was, and he is deceived, and then another complains of fate, of circumstances, of others, but never of himself, and yet at the bottom self is the only guilty person. This is why with the help of natural selfishness we weary all to whom we relate our misfortunes.[1]

You will understand better, gentlemen, the share of responsibility which belongs to unhappy married persons when I shall have spoken to you about the profanation of marriage. This profanation is the cause of the greater part of the evils complained of, which render the yoke of indissolubility

---

[1] Letter from Monsieur Alexandre Dumas to Monsieur Adrien Marx, quoted by *L'Univers*, October, 1886.

insupportable. If this yoke presses with too heavy a weight on guilty shoulders, is it right to call it barbarous? No—its rigor is justice. The law turns against those who have defied it, and becomes their chastiser. If they revolt against their chastiser, if they yield to temptation and end in crime, the law of indissolubility is no more responsible for this crime than is the law against theft for the assassination committed by a thief when he cannot take a purse without taking life.

Remark, I pray you, that in order to defy the law, it is not necessary to enter upon marriage with formally criminal intentions. It is sufficient that, blinded either by interest or passion, one should forget the grave duties which should be fulfilled with generous and holy resolutions. In this respect, I do not fear to say, there are but few to be found innocent among unhappy married couples. And even if there are some innocent ones among them, the law is not compelled to bend before their misfortune; for it is a general law, a law of great forethought, of superior interest, of individual perfection, domestic and social. It asks from the innocent the sacrifice of that happiness for which they had hoped. It is the hour for them to accomplish a great act of self-abnegation and devotion, just as it is the hour for the soldier to die on the battlefield when the safety of his country is at stake.

Do not refuse them this honor, do not break by sacrilegious license the great law of sacrifice on which the glory, and even the existence, of society depends. The law of sacrifice, no doubt, is hard to nature, and the innocent may ask why the law immolates them. But it is an element that must be remembered in this critical situation, it is the grace which God adds to this law to prevent the falling away of human nature. The Christian can bear the yoke of indissolubility; he is not crushed by it; for the more unhappy he is, the more active and efficacious becomes the grace of the Sacrament of Matrimony. It strengthens, sustains, consoles him, and teaches him the divine art of making his sufferings beneficial even to those who cause him to suffer. And on the ruins of all the happiness for which the poor heart had hoped, it makes him taste the severe and noble enjoyment of an immolation glorious before God and more useful to society than bloody sacrifices. As to those who will make no account of grace, we shall see, gentlemen, if it would be well to accept for them the remedy proposed to us by the opponents of the divine law.

II.

We have said that divorce is worse than all the evils for which men desire to make indissolubility responsible, and that it is, therefore, a principle of decay. No one has shown this truth more strikingly than the infallible doctor who governs the Church to-day, the Sovereign Pontiff Leo XIII., in his Encyclical on Christian Marriage. I desire only to be here the humble commentator on his word. Listen to it.

"One can hardly enumerate the great evils of which divorce is the source. The conjugal tie thereby losing its indissolubility, you must expect to see kindness and affection between husband and wife destroyed, an encouragement given to unfaithfulness, the protection and education of children rendered more difficult, germs of discord sown among families, the dignity of the wife ignored, the danger of her seeing herself deserted after having served as an instrument of the passions of man. And because nothing ruins families and destroys the most powerful kingdoms more than corruption of manners, it is easily to be seen that divorce, which is born only of the depraved customs of nations, is the most formidable enemy of families and of States, and, as experience affirms, it opens the door to the most vicious habits, both in private and in public life."[1]

Thus, then, gentlemen, according to the august words you have just heard, everything suffers

---

[1] At vero quanti materiam mali in se divortia contineant, vix attinet dicere. Eorum enim causa fiunt maritalia fœdera mutabilia; extenuatur mutua benevolentia; infidelitati perniciosa incitamenta suppeditantur; tuitioni atque institutioni liberorum nocetur; dissuendis societatibus domesticis præbetur occasio; discordiarum inter familias semina sparguntur; minuitur ac deprimitur dignitas mulierum, quæ in periculum veniunt ne, cum libidini virorum inservierint, pro derelictis habeantur.

Et quoniam ad perdendas familias, frangendasque regnorum opes nihil tam valet, quam corruptela morum facile perspicitur, prosperitati familiarum ac civitatum maxime inimica esse divortia; quæ a depravatis populorum moribus nascuntur ac, teste rerum usu, ad vitiosiores vitæ privatæ et publicæ consuetudines aditum januamque patefaciunt.
—Encyclic. *Arcanum divinæ sapientiæ.*

from divorce; marriage itself, those who marry, children, families, the whole of society.

Marriage as a contract that may be cancelled is no longer surrounded by those salutary precautions which should assure its peace and duration. In fact, it is no longer a question of establishing something, but of trying a venture in which rein may be given to every rashness and audacity. Of what use are all the searchings of delicacy and prudence, as it is no longer a question of settling one's self for life? If the ground on which we make the engagement is not solid, we will leave it to go elsewhere. It is useless to appeal to that deep and tender sentiment which unites hearts together and seeks and promises eternity; the appetite of sense is sufficient for him who only wishes to be bound for a time. Marriage is no longer the bringing together of two lives which confide in each other, complete and perfect each other in a permanent union; it is a terminable society, in which mistrust keeps all its rights, and, as it has been strongly remarked, it is a kind of legal prostitution to which man and woman give themselves up to become debased and degraded.

In short, whilst indissolubility elevates moral life, by obliging man to generous effort, to correct his nature and to bravely bear the annoyances of married life, divorce lowers him, because it binds him to nothing and gives full license to selfishness and caprice. We must make sacrifices if we would be amiable, gentle, kind, and obliging. But why should we do so? We need not fear to displease those of whose company we can rid ourselves. This prospect makes all restraint unnecessary, and leaves defects uncorrected. We clash, hurt, and lacerate ourselves until we can only say: life has become unbearable, let us separate.

In order to weary the husband or wife who is no longer desired contradictions and ill usage will be perfidiously exaggerated. What becomes of holy conjugal fidelity agitated by the constant desire of a rupture? The indissolubility of the marriage tie protects it against the temptations which allure love to another object. To the man tormented by an unlawful passion it says: "Take care, you no longer belong to yourself." Divorce, on the contrary, encourages the faithless heart and says to it: " Go where love calls you, you can resume your liberty." Since unfaithfulness is one of the chief causes of divorce, it is made a regular trade. Adultery is studied, plotted, and committed, in the damnable hope of securing a legal rupture of the conjugal tie.

It is thus man and woman, who might be so great and so noble under the law of indissolubility, are lowered and degraded under the law of divorce. Especially woman; woman, whose dignity Christianity has raised, and whom our fathers associated with their respect to their God and their king. Cursed, said they, be he who betrays his God, his king, or his wife! Woman is more than man the victim of the degradation which divorce entails. Man can withdraw from conjugal society with all the advantages of his strength and his authority in order to enter upon new ties; woman cannot withdraw from it with all her dignity. She leaves behind her best possessions, her maiden beauty and the charms of her youth, and only regains with difficulty the money she had brought. Who shall seek this withered plant, whose freshness is gone, and who is cast out from the family she has born, when she can no longer hope to found another? And if the woman is still young and full of life, and has herself provoked, under the influence of passion, the rupture of the tie that bound her to one love, what can she be in the eyes of the world? She is despised as an ungovernable woman, whose shame and disgrace are increased by each new union.

But the married couple are not the only sufferers from the dishonor and injustice of their separation. Divroce is an evil that exercises a sad and lamentable influence on the family and on society. It outrages the tie of blood which unites the child to its parents, and when it cannot break what nature has made indissoluble, it repudiates the most sacred obligations. It generally interrupts the important work of education at the very time when authority and persuasion, firmness and gentleness, should be closely united to perfect it. It snatches children from the place of their birth, transports them to strange places, and exposes them to the dislikes, rebuffs, and ill-treatment of new fathers and new mothers on whom they have no claim. It sows the seeds of contempt and hatred in young hearts where only respect and love should germinate, one taking the part of a mother unjustly abandoned, another the part of a betrayed father. It arms against each other whole families who espouse the cause of their blood; these exaggerate the faults of the guilty, those look for faults in the innocent. It provokes complaints, recriminations, and reproaches, multiplies discord, quarrels, and lawsuits.[1] Divorce disturbs public order and corrupts society. It corrupts society because it ruins the conservative and regulating principle of all social energy, the principle of authority. In submitting to the judgment of children the conduct of their father and mother, it lessens the value of the primitive power of the family, of which public power is only an imitation, a participation, a general application. It forms, little by little, generations impatient of every form of restraint, because they have learned to despise their parents and have had nothing before their eyes at the domestic hearth but the spectacle of license falsely labelled liberty. It cor-

---

[1] The happiness of the State lies in the peace and concord of citizens, in the good understanding between different families. Marriage, by uniting two persons, draws together parents, friends; by rendering two persons happy, it makes twenty friends. Divorce comes; it makes twenty mortal enemies. It excites the relatives, the friends of the wife against the husband, against his family' and his friends. Marriage had mingled their interests, strengthened their fortunes. Divorce comes to divide these interests, overturn their fortunes, raise discussions, provoke lawsuits, break testaments, and the courts of justice resound only with complaints against the husband who leaves his wife after having spent her fortune, and against the wife who leaves her husband, asking back what she has already wasted.—Barruel, *Letters on Divorce to a Deputy of the National Assembly*, 1788.

rupts society because it is the practical triumph of this execrable maxim: that in marriage it is permitted to consider less the stability of families than the liberty of pleasure, less the promises of love than the calculations of interest, less what is duty than what is passion.

Gentlemen, the conclusion from what you have just heard is self-evident. Divorce takes away from marriage its guarantee of delicacy, of prudence, and of love. Divorce crushes effort and progress in married life, and makes woman fall from the dignity to which eighteen centuries of Christianity have raised her. Divorce outrages the tie of blood and violates the rights of children. It disorganizes and divides families, disturbs public order, and corrupts society. Divorce is a principle of decay.

To those who may accuse me of making a merely hypothetical case, I reply: Take up history; you will read in it that same conclusion written in ill-omened letters in the life and in the death of every nation that violated the law of the indissolubility of the marriage tie. You will there see women crushed and degraded by the tyrannical power which man assumes when the right of repudiation is introduced into marriage. You will hear this piteous cry resounding on the stage of antiquity: "Of all the beings who live and have intelligence we women are the most miserable race."[1]

---

[1] Omnium autem quæcumque sunt animata et mentem habent, nos mulieres sumus miserrima propago.—Euripides, *Medea*.

History will show you that the grave Romans made wonderful progress as long as they put in practice this definition of conjugal society: "A community of divine and human law:" *Juris divini et humani communicatio.* You will remark that decay is hurried on by the fissure of divorce, which they had forgotten to close, and which the edicts of emperors widened. Divorce triumphs. There is an end of the respect with which the august matron was surrounded. This ornament of Roman society disappears. The matron is replaced by bad women, who reckon their years not by the number of the consuls, but by the number of their husbands,[1] who change households eight times in five years,[2] and are buried after having had twenty-two husbands.[3] The two sexes rival each other in inconstancy. Man only obeys his caprice and his passion. He sends away his wife, as one casts off a shoe that hurts the foot.[4] "Three wrinkles on the forehead, teeth whose enamel is tarnished, sunken eyes, a cold which remains too long, these suffice to separate him from the companion of his life and from the mother of his children. He does not even take the trouble to inform her of her repudiation; he sends her her bill of di-

---

[1] Numquid jam ulla repudio erubescit, postquam illustres quædam ac nobiles fœminæ, non consulum numero sed maritorum, annos suos computant.—Senec., *De Beneficiis*, lib. iii., cap. xvi.

[2] Si crescit numerus, sic fiunt octo mariti,
    Quinque per autumnos: titulo res digna sepulcri.
            Juvenal, *Sat.* VI., v. 229, 230.

[3] St. Jerome affirms having been witness of this fact.

[4] So said Paul Emilius, when sending away his wife Papyria.

vorce. Madam, pack up your goods and go. We can no longer tolerate you, you blow your nose too often! Make haste, the time is short. We are expecting another wife, who is not subject to cold in the head.[1]

The Roman patricians make exchanges among themselves; Cato gives up his wife to Hortensius; "it is the custom among noble people,"[2] says a historian. They only marry with the hope of divorcing; divorce is, as it were, a fruit of marriage."[3]

The law is altered many times without its being able to be made anything but an adulterous law.[4] Modesty has fled with religious marriage, and the same men and women who astonished the world by their chastity, now astound it by their laxity.[5] These debaucheries, fleeting unions, all either for pleasure or interest, disgust one with marriage and

[1] Cur desiderio Bibulæ Sertorius ardet?
Si verum excutias, facies non uxor amatur.
Tres rugæ subeant, et se cutis arida laxet,
Fiant obscuri dentes, oculique minores:
Collige sarcinulas, dicet libertus, et exi;
Jam gravis es nobis, et sæpe emungeris. Exi
Ocius, et propera; sicco venit altera naso.
  Juvenal, *Sat.* VI. v. 142-148.

[2] Quæ consuetudo vulgaris fuit.—Strabo, *Geograph.*, lib. vii. Tertullian (*Apologet.*) relates that Socrates gave up his wife Xanthippe to Alcibiades. In certain parts of Greece the husbands bartered with one another their wives.—Cf. Potter, *Archæolog. græc.*

[3] Repudium vero, jam et votum est, ut matrimonii fructus.—Tertul, *Apologet.*, cap. vi.

[4] The woman who marries so many times does not marry. Quæ nubit toties non nubit; adultera lege est.—Martial, *Epig.*, vi. 7.

[5] Proudhon, *On Justice in the Revolution and in the Church*, x. 19.

exhaust life. The population decreases, and Rome has not enough sturdy soldiers to defend her against the invasions of the barbarians. She borrows their forces and takes them into her pay. Vain precaution! Those whom she employs become enervated by contact with her corruption, and those who arrive newly from the frontiers of the empire end by stifling it.

Barbarians have conquered the world which divorce has corrupted. A new world is formed. The divine law of the indissolubility of marriage permeates it, fashions it, and creates the European society, which to-day is so full of life and power. But beware, gentlemen; Protestantism has reopened the terrible fissure of divorce through which decay is precipitated. Scarcely half a century after its appearance Germany complains of divorce as a premium of encouragement given to conjugal dissension.[1] Never, says a Protestant author, has one seen so many married people separated as in this extravagant century, decayed and approaching the end of the world, ... in which fools teach publicly the legitimacy and necessity of a plurality of wives."[2]

---

[1] I consider that never since the first ages of Christianity have separations and divorces been so common as in our day, since, after the example of Moses, we have thought to find therein a remedy for licentiousness It is greatly to be feared that in permitting divorce we have only given a premium of encouragement to conjugal dissension. —Schwenkfeld, Epist. ii. 1. (1538.) Cf. Döllinger, *The Reformation, its Development, and the Results it has produced in Lutheran Society*, vol. ii.

[2] Monner, *De Matrimonio*. (1561.)

England, converted at the Reformation by a lascivious king, is no happier. Divorce there multiplies domestic crimes to such a pitch that at the beginning of this century a prelate of the Anglican hierarchy is obliged to confess in open Parliament that, thanks to the law of divorce, unfaithfulness is become a kind of commerce, carried on for the benefit of discontented husbands and seducers.[1]

No doubt, gentlemen, in our Christian society decay is less rapid than in pagan society, and people have some modesty, which restrains them in the descent towards too great license. No thanks to their dispositions for this modesty and tardiness, but rather to the sacred law of indissolubility which protects them, and which no one shall abrogate so long as there are in this world a Church and Christian families.

Nevertheless, we are not safe from the catastrophes which corruption of manners infallibly brings. Hear the word of the Father of the faithful: " The greatness of the evils engendered by divorce will be better understood when it is borne in mind that the faculty of divorce once granted, no rein, however strong, can restrain it within just limits, not even within those which have been already fixed. The force of example is great; much great-

---

[1] In the discussions which took place not long ago in the English Parliament, the Bishop of Rochester, replying to Lord Mulgrave, asserted that out of ten demands for divorce on account of unfaithfulness, there were nine in which the seducer had agreed beforehand with the husband to furnish him with the proofs of his wife's unfaithfulness.— De Bonald, *Divorce in the Nineteenth Century*, etc., chap. xi.

er still is the force of passion. Then it must come to pass that, similar to a sickness propagated by contagion, or to a mass of water which has overflown its banks and spreads everywhere, this rage of divorce shall increase from day to day, and shall obtain influence over the majority of minds."[1]

That is the danger, gentlemen. If the children of God, weary of bearing the yoke of indissoluble union, permit themselves to be tempted by the too numerous examples of repudiation in which passion seeks its liberty; if human laws triumph over the divine law; if divorce becomes the custom of our society, there is an end to all: our decay is certain, more profound, and more shameful than any decay in history, because we shall have fallen from a greater height.[1] Divorce gives license to human lust, which is insatiable. After restraint of liberty, it desires unbounded liberty; after legal union, union at its own pleasure, and in this union polygamy, and after polygamy, promiscuousness. The do-

[1] Multoque esse graviora hæc mala constabit; si consideretur, frenos nullos futuros tantos, qui concessam semel divortiorum facultatem valeant intra certos aut ante provisos limites coercere. Magna prorsus est vis exemplorum, major cupiditatum: hisce incitamentis fieri debet, ut divortiorum libido latius quotidie serpens plurimorum animos invadat, quasi morbus contagione vulgatus, aut agmen aquarum, superatis aggeribus, exundans.—Encyclic., *Arcanum divinæ sapientiæ*.

[2] Ideoque nisi consilia mutentur, perpetuo sibi metuere familia et societas debebunt, ne miserrime conficiantur in illud rerum omnium certamen atque discrimen, quod est socialistarum ac communistarum flagitiosis gregibus jam diu propositum. Unde liquet quam absonum et absurdum sit publicam salutem a divortiis expectare, quæ potius in certam societatis perniciem sunt evasura.—Ibid.

mestic hearths will become only court-yards and kennels; and in the race formed by the decay inaugurated by divorce marriage will only be defined as the union of male and female for the propagation of animals formerly called the human species.

We have not come to this, gentlemen, thank God, and I hope we never shall. But to prevent it, all true Christians and sensible men must unite resolutely and make their choice between the principle of decay and the law of progress and perfection. In short, they must proclaim, by their lives more than by their discourse, that they will not separate what God has joined together: *Quod Deus conjunxit homo non separet.*

Conference IV.

Legislation on Marriage.

My Lord[1] and Gentlemen:—If the unfortunate were the only persons to complain of the rigor of the divine law on the indissolubility of the marriage tie they might be induced to listen to reason; but the libertines and the impious are more numerous. They are not content with complaining, they appeal to the secular power and call upon the State to modify the divine law of marriage, which they impiously call criminal and barbarous. And they do this—as is well known—in favor of their passions, and not in the interest of that civilization and humanity about which they make such a noise. It is not necessary that the summons to the State should be very threatening. The secular power has for a long time lent a willing ear to those protests which flatter its dormant ambition, and serve as an excuse to extend its dominion and power of legislation. Casuists and court theologians have materially helped the State to invade the domain of religion and conscience, and the sophists of naturalism have succeeded in persuading the State that it possesses all rights, and is the supreme power on earth.

[1] Monseigneur Richard, Archbishop of Paris.

There is nothing easier than to grant the demands of the impious and the libertines on the subject of marriage. Legislation is all that is needed. Marriage is simply "a contract for the benefit of the State and the good of society,"[1] and consequently it is the business of the State to ratify that contract, to regulate and modify its conditions according to the exigencies of the times and the conditions of the persons who make the contract. The State has the first right, the prior claim, to regulate marriage. The right of any religion or any Church to meddle is secondary. Those who marry are free to have the union which "the State regulates and effects"[2] blessed and sanctified by a religious ceremony, but they must expect the intervention of the State. And even after their union has been consecrated, they can always have recourse to State intervention, and make the laws and regulations of the religious society to which they belong bow before the laws and regulations of the State.

Behold, gentlemen, the pretensions of the secular power. It has thrust itself forward with so much audacity and persistency, it has been supported by so much sophistry, that it has ended by disturbing the public mind; and I would not be astonished if it had produced even in your Christian souls the strangest confusion with regard to legislation on marriage. Allow me to enlighten your consciences

---

[1] Portalis in *l'Exposé des Motifs*, presented to the French "Corps Legislatif" on the fifth title of the civil code and law on "Marriage."
[2] Ibid.

and to set in order your ideas on this important and delicate subject. In opposition to the pretensions of the secular power, I maintain that legislation on marriage, as to its very essence and essential properties, belongs to God and to His Church. This truth proved, I shall show you with what wisdom and with what power the Church proceeds in her legislation on matrimony.

I.

Let us retrace our steps, gentlemen, and place ourselves in the presence of the principle enunciated in our preceding conferences; that is to say, that all the power, all the reason of marriage, lies in the tie formed between man and woman by the mutual giving and accepting of their persons. "This tie," says St. Thomas, "is marriage itself, and it is always God Who makes it:" *Et talis relatio est semper a Deo.*[1] I ask myself how a human power can have the pretension to seize and to regulate this matter, so internal, so spiritual, so divine. That the State forget its nature is possible; but this forgetfulness gives it no right to intermeddle in a sacred action in which God is present as supreme master of the persons and lives which He binds to each other.

I know very well that people wish to see in marriage only a simple contract, similar to the contracts by which men exchange, transmit, engage their goods, their services, the fruits of their labor and their industry: all things in which the secular

---

[1] *Summ. Theol.*, suppl., quæst. 48., a. 2. ad. 2.

power may have a right of inspection and regulation, in the interests of order and public property; but this is a radically false idea, which vitiates all the practical consequences which may be drawn from it for the exercise of legislative power.

"If marriage is a contract," says Moser, "it is totally different both in its nature and substance from all other contracts:" *Quod naturam ac substantiam suam a reliquis contractibus toto cœlo differt.* Study its origin and what it is in itself, and you are obliged to confess that this truly singular contract has been instituted immediately by God Himself; that He has prescribed its rules, which no human power can either change or relax, and that He has taken the trouble to define in the Sacred Books the conditions which may render it valid or invalid. This is why St. Thomas calls it a spiritual contract; and from this it follows that the secular power, which can annul other perfectly valid contracts, and supplement, under certain conditions, the consent of the contractors, can do nothing and shall never be able to do any such thing when it is a question of marriage.[1]

[1] Matrimonialis contractus, abstractione etiam facta a ratione sacramenti, quoad naturam et substantiam suam a reliquis contractibus toto cœlo differt..... Qui matrimonii naturam atque originem attenta mente consideraverit, statim fateri cogetur contractum esse vere singularem, non ab hominibus sed a Deo ipso immediate institutum, circa quem varias quoque ipse præscripsit regulas a nulla potestate humana immutandas aut relaxandas: v. g. circa ejus unitatem, indissolubilitatem aliasque proprietates; item circa personas, quæ ad hunc contractum valide ineundum habiles aut inhabiles non existerent.—Gen. ii 28; Levit. xvii., xx.; Deut. xx., 22, 26.

Hinc matrimonium a St. Thoma contractus spiritualis appellatur

In fact, gentlemen, the secular power has no right over that which gives itself in marriage. Our fortunes, our fields, our houses, our labors, our services, border on other houses, other labors, other services; our temporal interests are combined with other interests, and we conceive that for public order, for the public good, the exterior acts, engagements, and contracts, by which all things enter into relationship, should be regulated by the secular power. But when man and woman, in taking hands, say to each other: I am thine, thou art mine, it is their person, their life, their liberty, their heart which they mutually give; sacred possessions bound together in the sacred intimacy of indissoluble union of marriage. By what right does a human power come and say to them, you shall not give yourselves, or you shall only give yourselves in such and such a manner?

My soul, my body, my person, is mine; my life, with all the energy with which God has endowed it, is mine; my liberty, which I bind, is mine; my heart, which I give to another heart, is mine. Yes, mine and God's. I wish to submit myself to His supreme jurisdiction in disposing of the possessions He has given to me; but I do not recognize, I will not recognize, any other jurisdiction. My sacred possessions, I do not place them in circula-

---

..... hinc quoque fit, quod publica potestas, quæ alios contractus, etsi valide initos, quandoque rescindere, item requisitum in contrahentibus consensum certis in conditionibus supplere valet, nihil tamen horum circa contractum matrimonialem præstare possit, nec unquam potuerit.—*De impedim. matrim.*, cap. xxiii., § 8, 9, 10, 11.

tion in the social life where the secular power makes laws and governs. I keep them for myself; for, in giving them to him or her whom I love, they are still mine, because God has said: "we are two in one flesh:" *et erunt duo in carne una.* The secular power has, then, nothing to look after when a man is giving himself in marriage; it has nothing to look after, either, in what he does when giving himself. What does he do? He makes a tie which binds his person, his life, his liberty, his heart to another person, another life, another liberty, another heart. Besides, this tie is an interior and spiritual bond which concerns only his conscience, and conscience is a sanctuary on whose gates is read: "Let the profane keep far from here!" *Procul hinc profani!*—The domicile which only shelters the body is already a sacred spot which the secular power cannot violate without drawing on itself the indignation and contempt of honest people, and yet it is desired that the State may enter into the conscience to see what is passing there, to fasten or unfasten at its fancy the tie which love makes.

The marriage tie is protected against the interference of the secular power by the facts that it is made by the joint wills of the man and the woman, and that, having made it, they cannot sever it. The ancients, as we remarked in our conference on the sanctity of marriage, called religion to the wedding, thus recognizing the intervention of a mysterious and supernatural power in the union of husband and wife. We see in the true history of the human family this supernatural power sealing with a solemn benediction the alliance of the couple who were the first parents of all families and all societies. Where were you, the State and the secular power, when God instituted marriage, and gave it the seal of His sovereign power? God, by determining the essence and fundamental qualities of marriage, wished to signify to you that the intimate union which should represent the marriage of His Word, and the multiplication of the race which should people His heaven with the elect, were things that concerned Him, and with which you have nothing to do. The family preceded you; it was constituted, united, and established by God, before men had thought of delivering to you the commission to govern in public matters, in order to teach you that marriage, in so far as it is a union, does not need your concurrence; that its essence is impenetrable and inviolable; that no human power can prevent the wills of man and woman from joining with the divine power, so as to form the conjugal tie; and that this tie once made, no human power can place it in the grasp of its legislation.

It follows from this, gentlemen, that marriage outside the Christian ordinance is what it can be, as to its essence and fundamental properties; this we have not to examine here; it is sufficient for us to know that, subject to the law of nature and to the law of God, it is independent of all civil law.

The incompetency of the secular power is still more manifest, if we enter upon the Christian ordinance, because we find ourselves face to face with a sacred thing, which cannot spring from any profane jurisdiction. Marriage is a sacrament. This sacrament has been the torment of jurists, whose jealous ambition cannot suffer near the secular power any independent power, even when it is God Who has constituted it. Their tendency to secularize religious things, in the question which now occupies us, has been encouraged by certain theologians of bad counsel, for whom the contract and the sacrament in marriage are two distinct things: the sacrament, a supernatural condition, added to the contract as to a thing finished and perfect of its kind.

If it should be thus, gentlemen, the victory would not be gained by the secular power, because we have proved to it that the matrimonial contract differs, as heaven from earth, from the other contracts on which it legislates. On the other side, if the secular power avows with some of its jurists that the contract of which the conditions are made by human laws can become the matter of a sacrament,[1] we reply that the matter of a sacrament is a sacred thing, of which a sacred power alone can determine the conditions. But we have no concessions to make on this point. The separability of the contract and of the sacrament is a grave error, against which the very na-

---

[1] This is the legal theology which is found in Pothier, *Contrat de Mar.*, t. i., chap. iii.: "The civil contract being the matter of the sacrament of marriage, there can be no sacrament of marriage when the civil contract is void."

ture of marriage, its divine institution, and the constant doctrine of the Church protest. I have expressed the fear that this error may have tarnished the opinion you yourselves have of marriage. It is time to give you the true doctrine on this subject.

It is impossible, gentlemen, to separate in practice two things which spring from one and the same cause as one and the same effect. Now, such are in marriage the contract and the sacrament. Christians who unite themselves are, as I have lately taught you,[1] invested by baptism with the power of making and giving a sacred thing. Their mutual tradition, their mutual acceptation, are joined and perfected like the matter and form in the other sacraments, and at the very instant that the conjugal tie is formed, grace springs forth, the sacrament is consummated. There are not here two causes, but one alone; not two acts, but one single act; and by the virtue of this single act the contract and the sacrament subsist as one single and indivisible thing. Even should you accept the opinion of those who despoil the contractors of their ministerial power to the advantage of the priest charged by the Church to bless and ratify their union, the things cannot be divided. You can no more separate the contract from the sacrament than you can separate civil contracts from the legal formalities on which their validity depends. The contract, powerless and informal matter, is incapable of effecting a union and

[1] Conference I., The Sanctity of Marriage, part ii.

of forming a tie, if it is not laid hold of by the sacred words which sanctify it. By itself, it can only be the incomplete element of an indivisible action, and it is identified with the sacrament in this one and only thing which is called Christian marriage.

This is what Christ desired when He sanctified by grace what God had blessed in the beginning of time. The efficacious sign of this grace is no new rite which He invents and adds to the matrimonial contract; it is the contract itself raised to the dignity of a sacrament, and so strong in this supernatural dignity, that no human power can any more break it: *Quod Deus conjunxit homo non separet.* Has not the Apostle St. Paul, explaining this mystery, said: "Man and woman shall be united by the exchange of their consent, and after that they shall be sanctified by a great sacrament," but then: "A man shall leave his father and mother, and shall cleave to his wife, and they shall be two in one flesh: Here is a great sacrament: *Sacramentum hoc magnum est*"?

Let all tradition be explored, there will not be found in it the smallest trace of the distinction imagined by canonists and court theologians for the use of jurists who flatter the ambition of the secular power. Depositary of a teaching which has never varied, the Church has condensed it in these few words, *Matrimonium est sacramentum:* "Marriage is a sacrament." I have explained to you, gentlemen, the sense of this brief and significant affirmation. It means, not that there is a sacrament above the contract or mixed with the contract, but that the sacrament is the contract itself; the contract invested by God with the power to produce grace, after the manner of all the sensible signs which He, as the supernatural Author, has made instruments of His power.

Besides, the Church has clearly expressed herself by the mouth of the Sovereign Pontiffs, every time she has had to pronounce on the doctrine of separation. "No Catholic," she says, "is ignorant, nor can be ignorant, that marriage is truly and properly one of the seven sacraments of the evangelical law instituted by Christ, and that there can be no marriage between the faithful without there being, immediately and at the same moment, a sacrament."[1] And again: "That is false doctrine, and worthy of condemnation, which asserts that the sacrament of marriage is only an accessory to the contract that can be separated from it, and that it consists simply of the nuptial benediction.[2]

Jurists have in vain attacked Christian marriage: they shall not snatch from it the contract, to make

[1] Cum nemo e catholicis ignoret, aut ignorare possit, matrimonium esse vere et proprie unum ex septem evangelicæ legis sacramentis a Christo Domino institutum, ac propterea inter fideles matrimonium dari non posse, quin uno eodemque tempore sit sacramentum.—Allocut. Pii IX. ad Patres Cardinales, die 27 Sept. 1852.

[2] Plura de matrimonio falsa asseruntur: Nulla ratione fieri posse Christum erexisse matrimonium ad dignitatem sacramenti: matrimonii sacramentum non esse nisi quid contractui accessorium, ab eoque separabile, ipsumque sacramentum in una tantum nuptiali benedictione situm esse.—'ius IX., *In Damnat. et Prohib. operis Joan. Nepom. Nuytz, Profess. Taurinensis, cui titulus: Juris Ecclesiastici Institutiones. J. N. Nuytz*, etc.

it a creature of the secular power; they shall not extract from it the grace of the sacrament, to reduce it to the condition of a purely civil agreement. Finally, between the contract and the sacrament there is more than a juxtaposition, more than a soldering, more than a penetration, there is identity: the cause of the contract being the cause of the sacrament; the obligation, the tie formed by the contract being what remains of the sacrament, that which theology calls the thing itself of the sacrament: *res ipsa sacramenti.*[1]

And now, gentlemen, listen to the conclusions drawn from this doctrine of inseparability and identity; they are serious and deserve to be remembered.

Christian marriage is a sacred thing; hence, its essence and its fundamental properties cannot be subject to legislative power of a purely human authority: hence, the efforts of the secular power to prevent the union of Christians would be useless: it can hinder nothing; hence, in vain it says to them: I unite you,—in the depths of their consciences it unites nothing; hence, it would endeavor in vain to break the sacred tie after they have united themselves: it can break nothing; hence, the sentences it pronounces in the cases which concern the essence and properties of marriage decide nothing; hence, should it meet with any of the faithful so forgetful of their baptism as to be

---

[1] Hujus procul dubio sacramenti res est ut mas et fœmina connubio copulati, quamdiu vivunt, inseparabiliter perseverent.—S. Aug., Lib. *De nuptiis*, cap. x., no. 11.

satisfied with the prohibitions, the consent, and the judgments of the secular power, whatever consideration they may enjoy among men, they shall not escape the opprobrium of hearing themselves called before the tribunal of God fornicators and adulterers.[1]

Do not exaggerate these conclusions. I am far from wishing to deprive the State of the power, and to forbid it every act of authority with regard to marriage. It has duties to fulfil and rights to exercise with regard to this venerable institution.

"Those who govern," says St. Augustine, "cannot serve the Lord except by forbidding and chastising with religious severity all that is contrary to His law."[2] A public power which understands its high mission should never lose sight of natural and divine law, in order to make its legislation agree with them. All respectable institutions, marriage among the rest, can only gain by this agreement.

But this noble use of the secular power with regard to natural and divine law does not prevent its asserting its rights over marriage, and it cannot be denied that it has them. St. Thomas states them with his customary precision. "Marriage," he says, "so far as it is a function of nature, arises from natural law;. in so far as it creates a commu-

---

[1] Quamlibet aliam inter Christianos viri et mulieris, præter sacramentum, conjunctionem, cujuscumque etiam civilis legis vi factam, nihil aliud esse, nisi turpem atque exitialem concubinatum.—Allocut. Pius. IX. sup. cit.

[2] Quomodo ergo, reges Domino serviunt in timore, nisi ea quæ contra jussa Domini fiunt, religiosa severitate prohibendo atque plectendo. —*Epist.* clxxxv. *ad Bonifac.*, c. x., no. 7.

nity, it is ruled by civil law; in so far as it is a sacred thing, it belongs to divine law."[1] It is on the side of nature and of the sacrament that we have met with the essence, the intrinsic properties, and the tie of marriage; we have placed all these things under protection from the assaults of the civil power. But the conjugal community entering into civil society, where it may be an element of trouble or of prosperity, it is impossible to withdraw it from the authority of those who have the mission to provide for public order, for the public welfare; and first, it is necessary to state its existence, and consequently to receive the declaration of the act which constitutes it. It is necessary, besides, to put in order the civil consequences dependent on this act, and the relations which it creates.

To prevent the decay and exhaustion of the physical strength of a nation, to avoid family troubles, scandals, and the sad consequences of capricious and immoral unions, to assure the performance of the public service, on which the security and preservation of a people depend, it may be necessary to create capabilities or incapabilities resulting from certain conditions of age, state, or consent. Hence questions of legal authenticity, of dowry, inheritance, succession, guardianship, admission to public functions, of civil legitimacy or illegitimacy, which might be the subject of a harassing, vexa-

---

[1] Matrimonium, in quantum est in officium naturæ, statuitur lege naturæ; in quantum est in officium communitatis, statuitur lege civili; in quantum est sacramentum, statuitur jure divino.—In IV. *Sent. Dist.* 34. a. 2. q. 1. ad. 4; Cf. Lib. iv. *Contra gentes.*, cap. lxxviii.

tious, unjust, tyrannical, and impious legislation, but also of a legislation both reasonable and salutary. Now, to this reasonable and salutary legislation the Christian should conscientiously submit. He incurs, at his own risk and peril, all its penalties, immediately that knowingly and voluntarily, in contempt of the law, he contracts a sacred engagement, over which the civil law has no hold and which it cannot invalidate.[1] But you will remark, gentlemen, that in the sphere where the legislative authority of the secular power is exercised, there can only be question of the civil condition and the civil consequences of marriage. The civil power legislates not on marriage itself, but around marriage ; not on that which is essential and principal in marriage, but on its accessories. The essence, the intrinsic properties, the tie of marriage transformed and elevated by Christ, are sacred things, which can only spring from a sacred authority.

[1] Formerly, in France, the marriages of the sons of a family contracted without the consent of their parents were void as to their civil consequences; that is to say, the contractors might be disinherited, the parents could legally compel them to restore the gifts which they had received before the marriage. Those who had assisted at the marriage were punished according to the will of the judge; the lives of the notary and the witnesses were in jeopardy. "After the dissolution of these marriages," says d'Héricourt (*Eccles. Laws*, part iii., chap. 5, *On Marriage*, § 76), "widows had neither dowry, nor recovery, nor any other matrimonial agreement; and the children who were born of this marriage, or who had been legitimatized by their means, were treated as illegitimate with regard to succession."

To-day, from a civil point of view, are considered illegitimate the unions of children made without the consent of their parents, of military men without the consent of their chiefs, and the unions of those who have not yet attained the age prescribed by law.

This authority, you have named it, gentlemen: it is the Church.[1] The secular power has desired to dispossess it; therefore it has imagined the doctrine of the separability of the contract and the sacrament. This ingenious discovery has made it bold; when rights are taken away, there is no hesitation about taking away too much. Having taken possession of the contract, the civil power desires to be its absolute master. Its hired theologians have not feared to define the strange dogma of the dependence of the Church on the consideration of the State in all matrimonial matters. This scaffolding of ambitious affirmations crumbles under the blows of the exposition you have just heard. We remain in the presence of a sacred thing, consequently in presence of the undivided power of the Church. It is Jesus Christ Himself Who has invested her with this power, for He has not in any respect separated marriage from the other sacraments of which He confided the dispensation to her. All divine mysteries must pass through her hands; she therein represents Christ Himself: *Sic nos existimet homo ut ministros Christi, et dispensatores mysteriorum Dei.*[2]

If the ministry of the Church is not immediate

---

[1] A conjugali fœdere sacramentum separi nunquam posse, et omnino spectare ad Ecclesiæ potestatem ea omnia decernere, quæ ad idem matrimonium quovis modo possunt pertinere.—Allocut., Pius IX., supra cit.

Cum matrimonium sit sua vi, sua natura, sua sponte sacrum, consentaneum est, ut regatur ac temperetur, non principum imperio, sed divina auctoritate Ecclesiæ, quæ rerum sacrarum sola habet magisterium.—Leo XIII. Encyclic. *Arcanum divinæ sapientiæ.*

[2] I. Cor. iv. 1.

in marriage, as in the other sacraments, it is certain that the contractors who act belong to her by baptism, and are subject to her sovereign authority. In keeping them, she keeps the entire sacrament; nothing can be done with it except according to her law. She binds, she looses, the contracting wills. Their consent cannot unite them if she prevents it; there are no further obstacles the moment she has said: speak. Where the tie is doubtful, she alone has the right to pronounce on its validity. If she decides that all is done well, they must remain united. They are free, if she says: it is ill done. Her penetrating authority can go to the very root of the conjugal union, heal the canonical vice of consent, and give it back all its efficacy. The sacred tie which cannot be broken either by the retractation of the act which made it or by the sentence of human justice, can be broken by her for the greater glory of God, or for the well-being of Christian society, when it has not yet been definitely established by the carnal union of husband and wife. And when she can do nothing with the very substance of the obligation contracted, she finds means to alleviate its rigor for the unfortunate, in suspending, by separation, the exercise of rights and the fulfilment of duties which have become an intolerable burden to them. You see, gentlemen, that, unlike human legislation, which moves around marriage, the legislation of the Church penetrates to its very essence, because marriage is a sacred thing, and the Church alone possesses a sacred power in the world.

This power the Church has exercised with supreme independence in those Christian societies which were formed under the jealous eye of pagan powers; she has maintained it in spite of all contradictions; she has defined it in those solemn articles of which I have not the time to explain to you the purport.[1] Spare me from quotations. I think I

---

[1] We add the following to the two definitions we have given above of the general power of the Church with regard to marriage:

First, the Canons of the Council of Trent, Sess. xxiv.

Can. III. Si quis dixerit eos tantum consanguinitatis et affinitatis gradus, qui Levitico exprimuntur, posse impedire matrimonium contrahendum et derimere contractum ; nec posse Ecclesiam in nonnullis illorum dispensare, aut constituere ut plures impediant et dirimant; anathema sit.

Can. IV. Si quis dixerit Ecclesiam non potuisse constituere impedimenta matrimonium dirimentia, vel in iis constituendis errasse; anathema sit.

Can. VI. Si quis dixerit matrimonium ratum non consummatum, per solemnem religionis professionem alterius conjugum non derimi; anathema sit.

Can. VIII. Si quis dixerit Ecclesiam errare, cum ob multas causas separationem inter conjuges, quoad thorum seu quoad cohabitationem, ad certum incertumque tempus fieri posse decernit ; anathema sit.

Can. XII. Si quis dixerit causas matrimoniales non spectare ad judices ecclesiasticos ; anathema sit.

Secondly, the contradictions of the propositions condemned by the Syllabus.

Prop. LXVIII. Ecclesia non habet potestatem impedimenta matrimonium dirimentia inducere, sed ea potestas civili auctoritati competit, a qua impedimenta existentia tollenda sunt.—Litt. apost. *Multiplices inter*, 10 Junii 1851.)

Prop. LXIX. Ecclesia sequioribus sæculis dirimentia impedimenta inducere cœpit, non jure proprio, sed illo jure usa, quod a civili potestate mutuata erat.—Litt. apost. *Ad apostolicæ*, 22 August, 1851.

Prop. LXX. Tridentini Canones qui anathematis censuram illis inferunt qui facultatem impedimenta dirimentia inducendi Ecclesiæ

have sufficiently proved that the intimate legislation on marriage belongs to the Church. I hasten to tell you with what wisdom and power the Church proceeds in her legislation on matrimony.

II.

You do not expect me, gentlemen, to enter into the details of the Church's legislation on matrimony, nor that I should draw from it practical applications. This study belongs to canon law and to casuistry. It is long, dry, complicated, necessary for those who should govern consciences; you do not need it. It is sufficient, in order to increase in your Christian souls respect for the sacred power with which the Church is invested, to show you that, after the manner of those legislators truly worthy of the name, she knows how to unite wisdom and power in the preventive, merciful, and punitive measures which she takes to protect and strengthen the venerable institution of marriage.

You may settle your life in it, but you cannot enter upon it as you will. There are on the road a succession of barriers which cannot be passed

---

negare audeant, vel non sunt dogmatici, vel de hac mutuata potestate intelligendi sunt.—Ibid.

Prop. LXXI. Tridenti forma sub infirmitatis pœna non obligat, ubi lex civilis aliam formam præstituat, et velit hac nova forma interveniente matrimonium valere.—Ibid.

Prop. LXXIV. Causæ matrimoniales et sponsalia suapte natura ad forum civile pertinent.—Ibid., Alloc. *Acerbissimum*, 27 Sept. 1852.

As to the power of the Sovereign Pontiff to dissolve a marriage ratified but not consummated, there is no other definition but the practice of the Holy See. We refer to the *Index* on this question.

without examination and permission. They are called impediments.

Superficial or evil-minded persons only see in these impediments a kind of toll by which the Church makes profit for the increase of her finances. The formidable multiplication of fiscal laws from which they suffer in civil life persuades them, no doubt, that one can scarcely have any power, even spiritual, without seeking to make money by it. Foolish prejudice, against which it is useless to argue; you are too reasonable not to estimate it rightly. Your serious minds seek in the measures taken by the most respected of all authorities the highest motives which can induce her to use her legislative power; and in company with all grave thinkers you believe that legislation on a sacred thing cannot be lightly made, nor from base motives, and that the impediments to marriage must have their philosophy.

You are right, gentlemen, the Church has multiplied the preventive measures of her matrimonial legislation only in the interests of those who marry, of the family, and of society. To the impediments imposed by the strength of natural law, she had added those which she believed to be necessary to assure the peace and holiness of the conjugal union, together with its liberty and its end.[1]

[1] To help the memory, rather than to satisfy literary taste, the fifteen diriment impediments are enumerated in the following lines:

"Error, conditio, votum, cognatio, crimen,
Cultus disparitas, vis, ordo, ligamen, honestas,
Amens, affinis, si clandestinus et impos,
Si mulier sit rapta, loco nec reddita tuto."

Marriage being of all the engagements which man contracts with his fellow-creature the most elevated, most delicate, most intimate, most irrevocable, nature desires that in it the will shall be perfectly free. Insanity or imbecility, which envelop it in darkness; error, which leads astray its choice; violence and rape, which falsify and constrain its resolutions, are so many obstacles which it is impossible to overleap before arriving at the union of consent and at the formation of the conjugal tie. The Church does not create them, she is satisfied to point them out. But her wisdom, profoundly respecting liberty, goes much further; she eliminates from marriage the servile condition which places a man in the power of another man. It does not satisfy her that those who marry should give themselves to each other, they must possess each other freely, and no stranger will can tyrannically oppose itself to the exercise of their respective rights. It is thanks to this wise character of its law that the Church has obtained from Christian masters the greater part of the emancipations which have destroyed slavery little by little, and have created our free society, in which the impediment of condition no longer exists.

The liberty of marriage being assured, it must be able to attain its humanitarian and social design: the propagation of the human species and the fusion of families into that great society which is called a people. For this reason, after having forbidden marriage to the unfortunate whose nature is incomplete, or whose energies lie dormant, the

Church further debars those from marrying who are too nearly related to each other. She says, as well as physiologists, that two bloods too nearly related in their source are with difficulty prolific; that their similarity predisposes them to pathologic inheritance, that is to say, to the sad transmission of the infirmities and maladies which afflict a family; that, like two poles of electricity, two bloods coming from afar combine more easily, and cause the spark of life to spring forth more vigorously; and, definitely, that man should not have less solicitude for the health and beauty of his noble race than he has for the health and beauty of the animal races which he makes use of for his nourishment and service. She forbids, then, not only those unions which are repugnant to nature, but she extends her prohibitions to those inferior degrees of relationship where she perceives a danger, should it be only that of the great concentration of families among themselves, of creating in society a kind of caste, in which the affections remain entrenched, or where possessions are amassed while life is impoverished. The foreseeing wisdom of the Church, according to the thought so beautifully expressed by St. Thomas, desires that marriage, pursuing its design to the end, may attain these two great social blessings: the confederation of men and the multiplication of friendships. It is with this design that she extends her prohibitions of consanguinity to affinity, in order that social union may result from the double diffusion of life and love.

To these guarantees from without are added

the guarantees of security and domestic peace, which permit husband and wife to live together without fear and trouble. The Church does not wish a man or woman to profit by a crime in order to be united to the accomplice of their passion. By shutting the doors of conjugal society to homicide and adultery, she takes from them all hope of obtaining their vile designs, and stifles in the germ many bold undertakings which would compromise the security of the domestic hearth.

But the Church's greatest anxiety is for the peace of souls. Love, so ardent in early days, grows lukewarm with time, and disparity of worship, forgotten for a moment, may, with its desires, its exactions, its susceptibilities, become a source of interminable discussion, bitter reproaches, and perhaps of incurable hatred. The Christian hearth is a sanctuary where before all else religious peace should reign ; and for that there must be but one faith, one God, one altar, one worship, as there is but one Baptism. Do not forget, gentlemen, that marriage is holy, and already the Church watches over its holiness, by proscribing a disparity of worship. But still more severe and more pure are her exactions with regard to this characteristic property of Christian marriage. It ceases to be holy and becomes sacrilege if it is made to the detriment of a right acquired by God. Also the Church considers that the sacerdotal character and solemn vows of religion are on the part of man gifts, on the part of God an entering into possession which does not permit other engagements.

More than that, gentlemen; the Church does not suffer the rights acquired by man to be violated. Not only does she arrest at the doors of the sanctuary those who would marry a second time before the tie which binds them be broken by death, but also those who, having given their word in solemn espousals, dare to brave public honesty by a kind of perjury. To such a degree is the Church jealous for the sanctity of marriage, that she does not permit that the union of her children should be suspected of any infamy, nor that secrecy should be abused to beguile their good faith and to extract from them a consent for which they would blush. Therefore she compels them, under pain of only producing powerless consent, to come out from clandestine shades, and in broad daylight to pronounce before her their oaths, and to receive her benediction.

Gentlemen, be the Church accused as much as may be of annoying those who marry in spite of her impediments, it is not less true, as you have just seen, that all her legislation is made in the interests of liberty, of the multiplication and health of human generations, of social unity, of the security and peace of the domestic hearth, of purity of faith, of the laws of God, of the laws of man, of the honor and good reputation of marriage itself. If it pleases the Church to moderate as much as she can the rigor of her legislation, she has certainly the right to exact some compensation. It is more than thanklessness and ill humor: it is folly, ingratitude, injustice, to profit by the dispensations which her merciful kindness grants to our weakness and our needs, while we attack her wisdom.

The wisdom of the Church, however, with all her preventive measures, would not have saved marriage from the attempts made by passion during eighteen centuries to deprave it, if she had not brought all her strength to the aid of her legislation. You have heard her protest with a loud voice against the unholy laws by which the emperors endeavored to prolong the immoral liberties of paganism, and you have heard her proclaim that the decrees of Cæsar are struck powerless by the decrees of God. Her courageous resistance has made yield around her those codes and customs contrary to her sacred laws, and she has arrived at combining in her law the matrimonial law of those nations who receive her Baptism.

But after having triumphed over the opposition of laws, it was necessary to combat the licentiousness of the great. For them, relationship and engagements made counted for nothing, directly there was a question of serving some interest or gratifying some passion. Publicly wicked, they would quickly have brought the Christian world back to the licentious manners which before them dishonored marriage, if the Church had not cried out to them, as John the Baptist did to Herod: *Non licet,* " It is not lawful," and if she had not crushed with the thunder of her censures their proud pretension to place themselves above laws.

Only in our own land, how many kings and

princes the Church has had to solemnly warn and strike without pity, when they revolted against her maternal admonitions. Theodbert, the grandson of Clovis, Clotaire I., Caribert, Dagobert, Childeric d'Austrasie, Pepin d'Heristal, Charlemagne himself, Lothaire, Robert the Pious, Philip I., Louis VII., Philip Augustus, and many princes and lords of less power. Not only among us, but all around us, the Church has had to make war with wickedness and divorce among crowned heads.

To excommunicate the guilty, brave their anger, place their kingdoms under interdict, shut the temples and cemeteries, absolve the people from their oath of allegiance, provoke their murmurs and cause their tears to flow, no cost was too great to obtain the victory over the scandal. In these struggles between the divine law and human passions a good number of bishops have sacrificed their lives, and the Church herself has preferred to have her bosom torn and her members cut off, rather than compromise by concession the holy cause of marriage. Railers have laughed at her excommunications, and the wise of the world have exclaimed at the scandal. Strange scandals are these repeated acts of spiritual vigor, which chastise crime and stifle it before it becomes contagious.

Without the courage and power which the Church has displayed in maintaining her legislation on marriage, the licentiousness of monarchs would have been imitated by their courts; from the court it would have passed to the people, and the public manners of Christian nations, like those of antiquity, would have offered to-day to our eyes only the repugnant spectacle of a universal putrefaction. For, be well persuaded, gentlemen, the holy laws of marriage are not violated with impunity: God is always ready to avenge them. We have seen sovereign races become extinct in the offspring whose birth the people had greeted with enthusiasm, and hope deceived has sought for the cause of these providential extinctions. There was perhaps no other cause but that of unions contracted in contempt of the laws of God and of the Church. Nations will become extinct like families in the day when they no longer respect these laws, in the day when the Church shall have no power to make their corrupt heart understand this holy precept of the Apostle, in which is summed up all her legislation on matrimony: "Marriage honorable in all, and the bed undefiled:" *Honorabile connubium in omnibus, et thorus immaculatus.* [1]

---

[1] I. Heb. xiii. 4.

CONFERENCE V.

The Profanation of Marriage.

MY LORD[1] AND GENTLEMEN:—The conclusions of our last conference completely overthrow the calculations of those who count on the civil power to reform the indissolubility of the marriage tie. The civil power can do nothing, for the question is not about a civil act but about an essential property of marriage. The Church is invested with divine authority, and she alone has the right to legislate on marriage. The Church, as the supreme teacher, is the only power that can pronounce practically on the value of the conjugal tie. If the tie is made as it should be, she has no authority, no commission from God to undo it, and those who complain of rigor must be satisfied with the answer contained in these words of the Saviour: *Quod Deus conjunxit homo non separet:* "What God hath joined together let no man put asunder."

Gentlemen: I have not forgotten the bitter pleadings with which the adversaries of the divine law on the indissolubility of the marriage tie have wearied us. I repeat their complaints for the express purpose of proving to you that the greater number suffer from the law because they have

---

[1] Monseigneur Richard, Archbishop of Paris.

outraged it, and because they have made it in their own cases the chastisement of a profanation.

Marriage, according to its primitive destination, should be an honorable and happy union: but into it, as into everything, sin has entered. St. Paul, who calls it "a great mystery," does not fail to tell us that we must expect to meet with tribulations therein: *Tribulationem habebunt.*[1] The imperfections and vices of our fallen nature can render these tribulations so numerous and so strong that it would be folly to confront them under an indissoluble yoke, if God had not prepared compensations for those who marry, in the three great blessings which theology calls: *Proles, fides, sacramentum.*

"*Proles,*" that is to say, the honor and happiness of living again in one's children, enriching the world with new beings, and of preparing an elect race for heaven.

"*Fides,*" that is to say, the sweetness, the consolations of a faithful intimacy into which one retires to make life's joys more real, or to withstand the blows of evil fortune.

"*Sacramentum,*" that is to say, the grace of the sacrament which strengthens the conjugal tie, heals the infirmities, or repairs the follies of nature.

"There must be nothing less than these three great blessings," says St. Thomas, "in order to excuse marriage, and to make it honorable:" *Hæc*

---

[1] I. Cor. vii. 28.

sunt bona quæ matrimonium excusant et honestum reddunt.[1]

Now, gentlemen, who are they who with candor, sincerity, and a spirit of faith seek the three great blessings of marriage? They are few. And when they have been deceived, when they suffer, they do not complain, believe me, because they cannot begin again their matrimonial experience by a new deception. As to those who ask for themselves or others this experience, I maintain that they do not deserve that the law should bend before their misfortune; for they suffer by their own fault, because they have all some dishonesty to reproach themselves with on account of one of the blessings of marriage, perhaps with regard to them all at the same time.

We shall make a study of modern marriages. It will be more useful and more convincing than all arguments, as a reply to those who meddle with the reformation of marriage, instead of condemning those who profane it.

I.

The fecundity of living beings is, in nature, the accomplishment of a precept of God, and it is the fruit of His benediction. The Lord said, "Increase and multiply:" *Crescite, multiplicamini;* and life spread through the whole universe, of which it is the ornament and the glory. Wherever it is absent, nature is cheerless and desolate; every-

---

[1] *Summ. Theol.*, suppl. quæst. 49. a. 1.

where that it abounds, we recognize and bless the paternal hand of God.

But in the little world of the human family, more than in the great world of nature, fecundity is a blessing. God has promised it to those whom He loves. He showed to His servant Abraham the stars of the firmament, which the children of his race were to equal in number.[1] He has inspired His prophets to sing the happiness of the man who fears the Lord: All prospers in his industrious hands. His wife beside him is like the fertile vine on the sides of his house, and his numerous children surround his table, joyful and full of hope, like the young shoots of the olive tree. He shall see his childrens' children: it is thus that God gives His blessing: *Ecce sic benedicitur homo.*[2] Yes, it is thus that God blesses; and when He wishes to curse, He denies posterity or destroys it. The posterity of the sinner be cut off, He says; in one generation may his name be blotted out: *Fiant nati ejus in interitum: in generatione una deleatur nomen ejus.*[3]

How beautiful is the smile of childhood! It is like a ray of sunshine at the hearth, and the more smiles there are, the more resplendent is the hearth. Multiply, charming beings, fill the house where

---

[1] Eduxitque eum foras, et ait illi: Suspice cœlum, et numera stellas, si potes. Et dixit ei: Sic erit semen tuum.—Gen. xv. 5.

[2] Labores manuum tuarum quia manducabis, beatus es et bene tibi erit. Uxor tua sicut vitis abundans, in lateribus domus tuæ. Filii tui, sicut novellæ olivarum, in circuitu mensæ tuæ. Et videas filios filiorum tuorum.—Psalm cxxvii. 2-6.

[3] Psalm cviii. 13.

you are born with your shouts and joyous animation; God loves to see you and to hear you. The Providence of little birds and of the lilies of the field, He desires especially to be the God of large families. He keeps in reserve for them His best blessings, and gives them inexpressible charms, which draw towards them the sympathy, the pity, and the generosity of benevolent hearts. There you will find none of that dull silence which saddens empty hearths; there, the hearts of parents are not exposed to that foolish idolatry which is seen growing around an only child; the number does not divide the love, it multiplies it; there are no irreparable absences, no mourning that cannot be consoled; the flower that God gathers leaves behind it lovable sisters, who are loved the more, as if to avenge the treason of death; there, work, devotion, sacrifice, are imposed and perpetuated in glorious and sacred tradition; there, are elect to people heaven; soldiers, to serve the country; pioneers, to take possession of the world. The empire of the earth belongs to large families: *Crescite, multiplicamini et replete terram.*

A Christian who understands this, and who knows how to enter into the designs of God, prepares with a deep respect for himself for the honor of paternity, and when the hour is come for him, he says to God, like the young Tobias: "Lord, Thou knowest that not for fleshly lust do I take my sister to wife, but only for the love of posterity, in which Thy name shall be blessed forever and ever." And he rejoices to hear fall on the head of her whom he has taken for a companion this blessing of the Church: "May she be fertile in children:" *Sit fœcunda in sobole.*[1]

And is it to be expected that God will bestow His blessing on sinfully restricted families as upon those where fecundity obeys the laws of nature? That cannot be; against the violators of His law God prepares a terrible revenge. He allows those who have deceived Him to enjoy for a time the fruit of their parsimonious fecundity. And when their heart is engrossed, when they have centred all their hopes with all their love in the only son or in the two little creatures to whom they have restricted their family,—death, the sad messenger of Divine Justice, comes to knock at the door of their home, and carries off, in spite of their cries and their prayers, those who leave behind them neither brothers nor sisters to console for their loss.

Again, it is better for God to punish quickly, for His vengeance delayed would become perhaps more terrible. The only child, the object of an idolatrous worship, opens its soul to all the passions bound together by a monstrous selfishness. Allow him to grow up; neither the warnings, nor the tears, nor the threats of those who have too fondly loved him can arrest his unbridled course on the road to perdition, at the end of which, victim of debauchery or of some shameful catastrophe, he will leave to his unfortunate parents a cursed

---

[1] Et nunc, Domine, tu scis quia non luxuriæ causa accipio sororem meam conjugem, sed sola posteritatis dilectione, in qua benedicatur nomen tuum in sæcula sæculorum.—Tob. viii. 9.

remembrance, to which they can only give utterance in this cry of despair: Love, hope, fortune, honor, all are lost!

Afterwards, if there are regrets, groans, tears, and reproaches for the hearth desolated by the justice of God, whose fault will it be? I have more than once been the sorrowful witness of this desolation, which is only increased by powerless desires. They would replace the children that are no more, but the time is past, or perhaps God is opposed to it. And then they imagine that other unions would be happier; they are irritated at the inflexible law which holds two sterile lives enchained; but the law, holy and just, does its work: it chastises those who have outraged it. This chastisement is their due, not only because they have offended God and cheated nature, but also because they have betrayed their country.

All public men who are anxious about the fate of nations keep an open eye on the census of the families of which they are composed. The more numerous these families, the greater the true riches of a nation; for the chief of all riches is life, is strength; and these only increase in order to invade and take possession of the world. God has willed it thus; He said to the first human pair: "Increase, and multiply, and fill the earth:" *Crescite, multiplicamini et replete terram.* Such is the law: the empire of the world belongs to prolific nations. They may be, perhaps, less polished than others, coarse, barbarous; but what does it matter? They possess in their generous blood that with which they may become masters. If the country where they swarm is too narrow for them, like the laborious bees, they take their flight towards other countries. The Old and the New World, continents and islands, are peopled by their emigration. Everywhere they lay hold of unoccupied land, everywhere they accumulate fertile generations, everywhere they stand ready to replace those peoples who become extinct.

These latter again deceive the eye by a factitious prosperity. By lessening families, they inflate individual fortunes; they create a current of business, of luxury, of pleasure, and I know not what refinements of civilization they mistake for life. But true life is exhausted in those abject calculations which limit fecundity. Where there is fear of children, there the population decreases. Where the population decreases, it is seen to clutch with selfish avidity its share of the possessions augmented by vacancies, and soon there are neither enough strong chests nor enough generous hearts to oppose innumerable and needy legions which prolific nations hurl against a sterile people. So that, if extinction is not produced by the blow of a warlike invasion, it will be the result of pacific infiltration. The country whose population decreases, incapable of sufficing by itself for the exigencies of its languid and vitiated life, allows itself to be invaded by degrees by strangers who send it their surplus. Yesterday they were hundreds, to-day they are thousands, to-morrow they will be millions. And by the force of multiplying they will fill the hospitable land where their swarms have settled down, and will take the place of the people who would not increase.

Do you not feel that it is so? Ah! pardon me. For a long time this idea has haunted me like a nightmare, and I ask myself whether at this hour there is not a people to whom God might say, as the aged Jacob said to his son: "Ruben, my first-born, thou art my strength, and the beginning of my sorrow; excelling in gifts, greater in command. Thou art poured out as water, grow thou not."[1] God grant that I may be mistaken!

II.

We have just seen how marriage is profaned in its chief blessing. There is yet another, without which married life becomes a torment, and which must be assured at all costs: fidelity. Fidelity is made up of love, of esteem, of confidence, and of sincerity. It is founded, not upon external gifts, which time and circumstances may alter, but upon the solid gifts of the mind, which experience strengthens and emulation perfects. It lives on open-hearted and loving confidences. It applies itself with generosity and devotedness to share in solicitude, labor, and suffering. It has pity for weaknesses and failings; it pardons faults and soothes wounds. It is prudent, discreet, and likes not to be suspected. In short, it binds hearts to-

[1] Ruben primogenitus meus, tu fortitudo mea et principium doloris mei; prior in donis, major imperio. Effusus es sicut aqua, non crescas.—Gen. xlix. 3, 4.

gether, and renders the conjugal union as happy as it can be, the imperfections of our poor nature being taken into account.

What a great blessing! The wise, the Christian man will make sure that he has it.

The Christian prepares for marriage by the apprenticeship of virtue, which every faithful heart should practise. His love is a delicate and precious flower, whose splendor, grace, and perfume he reserves for one only feast. No one shall know it, no one shall touch it, no one shall inhale its mysterious odor, before the virgin who shall possess it entirely. Obedient to the counsels of divine wisdom, he will give no woman power over his soul.[1] His modesty, his reserve, his generous effort will allow him to leave none of his honor and his strength there where so many unhappy young men have miserably given way. It is from God that he expects the companion of his life, and he desires to have merited her, for the prudent and good woman is the recompense of the just for all the good he has done.[2]

Above all human advantages, he seeks the divine advantages of his union. Instead of a fortune, which adversity overturns, instead of deceptive charms and vain beauty, which time withers, he prefers virtue. Men may deceive him; before asking

---

[1] Non des mulieri potestatem animæ tuæ.—Ecclus. ix. 2.

[2] Domus et divitiæ dantur a parentibus, a Domino autem proprie uxor prudens.—Prov. xiv. 41.

Pars bona mulier bona, in parte timentium Deum dabitur viro pro factis bonis.—Ecclus. xxvi. 3.

them for information, he takes counsel of God, and he learns in the Sacred Scriptures that the object of his desires, " is the courageous woman, whose price is beyond that of the most precious treasures, and who can receive into a steadfast heart the confidence of a manly heart;[1] it is the wise woman, who buildeth her house;[2] the diligent woman, who is the crown of her husband;[3] it is the gentle woman, who fills with joy the heart of her husband, and doubles the number of his years;[4] it is the industrious woman, who eats only the bread she has gained;[5] it is the simple woman, who despises the ridiculous use of paint and overloading with ornaments, and an exaggerated attention to dress;[6] it is the loving, prudent, chaste, sober, careful, kind, submissive woman, who not only never gives occasion to blaspheme the sacred word of God, but also never gives occasion to doubt her adorable goodness.[7] When the Christian man has found her, he exclaims: Spouse of my soul, " many daughters have gathered together riches, thou hast

---

[1] Mulierem fortem quis inveniet? Procul et de ultimis finibus prætium ejus. Confidit in ea cor viri sui.—Prov. xxxi. 10, 11.

[2] Mulier sapiens ædificat domum suam. —Ibid. xiv. 1.

[3] Mulier diligens corona est viro suo.—Ibid. xii. 4.

[4] Mulieris bonæ beatus vir; numerus enim annorum illius duplex.— Ecclus. xxvi. 1.

[5] Consideravit semitas domus suæ, et panem otiosa non comedit.— Prov. xxxi. 27.

[6] Quarum non sit extrinsecus capillatura, aut circumdatio auri, aut indumenti vestimentorum cultus.—I. St. Pet. iii. 3.

[7] Adolescentulos ut viros ament, filios suos diligant, prudentes, castas, sobrias, domus curam habentes, benignas, subditas viris suis, ut non blasphemetur verbum Dei.

surpassed them all:" *Multæ filiæ congregaverunt divitias, tu supergressa es universas.*¹ And how happy he is in seeing her so beautiful with true beauty, she who, having prepared herself in retirement, prayer, and pious waiting on the will of God, is happy to love in him a wise man, who has kept for his spouse the treasures of a spotless life; a courageous man, who will know how to protect her weakness; a true child of God, who will be the kindest of masters and the tenderest of friends. They suit each other, they love each other, they unite their hands and their hearts, and offer to God, with religious respect, the consent which binds them together. They have entered into marriage by the gate of wisdom; they will remain in it under the guard of fidelity.

Alas! we may say of the gate of wisdom what Our Lord said of the gate of heaven: *Quam angusta porta! .... quæ ducit ad vitam! et pauci sunt qui inveniunt eam:*² Narrow gate! There are few who find it. For the few consolations which Christian marriage gives us, how many are the unfaithfulnesses which sadden us! They arise, to begin with, from the profanations of those of whom the Angel Raphael said to young Tobias: "Who in such manner receive matrimony, as to shut out God from themselves, and from their mind, and to give themselves to their lust, as the horse and mule, which have not understanding."³

---

¹ Prov. xxxi. 29.   ² St. Matt. vii. 14.

³ Hi namque qui conjugium ita suscipiunt, ut Deum a se et a sua mente excludant, et suæ libidini ita vacent, sicut equus et mulus, quibus non est intellectus. — Tob. vi. 17.

The beauty of the flesh allures them, and as if bewitched by the charms which speak to their senses, they see no farther. Are there virtues or vices under the fragile mantle which time will destroy? They do not wish to think about that. Marriage is for them only a voluptuous feast, of which they forget the perpetual day following, full of deceptions and stern duties.

But they are not alone in defying the future. "Wide is the gate, and many there are who go in thereat:" *Lata porta, et multi sunt qui intrant per eam.*[1]—It would be vain to seek in their hearts for a spark of that true love, which alone can bind together, and forever, two human lives; interest, vanity, levity, insincerity, are to-day the too common agents in matrimonial unions.

This man wishes to quit an honest mediocrity, where his ambition is ill at ease, or he desires to remake an injured fortune. The dowry has for him sovereign charms, which eclipse all beauty, and advantageously replace all theological and moral virtues.

That woman blushes for the humble condition whence her family has risen, and for the honest toil which has made her an enviable heiress. To hide her common origin, and to give her vanity a right to wear the insignia of nobility, she marries a name and a title without being anxious to possess a heart.

Here, parents and children hurry a marriage, as if it were a question of bringing about the end

[1] St. Matt. vii. 13.

of the world. No one thinks of demanding from the past pledges for the future, nor of fathoming souls in order to measure their dispositions and virtues. An interview is sufficient to make them think they understand each other, and on the faith of superficial convenience two lives, almost strange to each other, are condemned from that day forward to meet in the most delicate and most awful of intimacies.

Criminal levity, often mingled with notorious insincerity; every one conspiring to deceive; some hiding defects, others concealing infirmities; these giving a false importance to lessened fortunes, those covering with false appearances vices artificially allayed and ready to re-awaken as soon as they shall have doubled the cape of wedlock.

I will not enter into the details of all the motives and influences which make modern marriage a captivation of the senses, an affair of money, a satisfying of pride, an undignified contract, a disloyal compact; but rest assured that on the vast arch under which the greater part of married people pass may be written in capital letters: Passion, Interest, Vanity, Levity, Insincerity.

After this, is it to be wondered at that sensual love wounds the delicacy of chaste love, and that there should be in marriage such disenchantment, such loss of affection, such contempt, which date from the day when an inconstant man has been without respect and without pity for maiden modesty? Is it to be wondered at that beautiful women without virtue should be extravagant, that others desire them, and that they make themselves to be desired? Is it to be wondered at that women who are taken for their money do not give their hearts; that men who are married for their name and their title are not loved? It is to be wondered at that hasty unions are badly cemented; that souls who have not been scrutinized should show themselves in intimacy under a repulsive aspect; and that persons who are scarcely acquainted should forsake each other, when they see their moral deformities? Is it to be wondered at that defects, infirmities, failings, vices, about which they did not wish to think, or which cunning and falsehood disguised, suddenly reveal themselves, to the great detriment of domestic peace and happiness? Is it to be wondered at that we see burst forth in daily life suspicions, jealousies, repugnance, contempt, disgust, anger, hatred, rancor? Finally, is it to be wondered at that unfaithfulness has installed itself in the home where passion, interest, vanity, levity, insincerity have enviously conspired against the great blessing of fidelity?

Yet again, I see bitter regrets, I hear murmurs and reproaches. They complain of being crushed under the inflexible yoke of the indissolubility of the conjugal tie; but whose fault is it? The guilty person is not God Who offers His counsel in the great business in which human life is engaged, and Who, in fact, has only made a law of progress and perfection. The guilty one is man, who has taken counsel only with his evil instincts and his folly, and who, knowing the law, has defied its holy rigors. If he suffers, I pity him; but I cannot abstain from saying with the Psalmist: "Thou art just, O Lord, and Thy judgment is right:" *Justus es Domine, et rectum judicium tuum.*[1]

Gentlemen, you will understand better the just reprisals of the divine law if you will consider with me how the best and most sacred of all the benefits of the conjugal union, the sacrament, is treated to-day.

III.

The prudent measures which human wisdom, led by the spirit of God, takes, are for the Christian a precious guarantee of the solidity, peace, and prosperity of his marriage. Nevertheless, in the most honest and well assorted souls nature has its outbursts, and can make its imperfections so keenly felt, as to seriously menace the peace of married life. Against these accidents God has placed safeguards in order to justify fully the severity of the law of which He has revived the inflexible rigor for Christian generations. He has raised marriage to the dignity of a sacrament, the virtue of which continues together with the conjugal tie.

"This sacrament," say St. Thomas, "is the most important of all the benefits of marriage, for it gives grace, more worthy than nature, and stronger than she is to cement the union of those who marry."[2]

---

[1] Ps. cxviii. 137.

[2] Proles et fides pertinent ad matrimonium, secundum quod est in

I will not repeat what I have already said about the efficacy of grace in marriage.[1] By perfecting natural love, by rendering it wise, patient, just, merciful, pure, and faithful in duty, it draws hearts together in such a manner that nothing shall evermore separate them. It is especially in the religious life of husband and wife that its unitive strength is manifested. Their heart is resplendent with the light of faith, and the peace of God reigns there. They believe the same truths; they adore, they love, they pray to, they serve together the same God, the same Christ Who has blessed them; they invoke Him to share in their joy; they find consolation for their troubles at the foot of the cross, which they clasp in their embrace; they share in all labor and adversity as well as in all happiness. The religious unity of their life serves as an example to the family which is born of their sacred love.

Behold the effect of grace! But who are they who receive it? In many cases, beside a believing and truly Christian soul there kneels a soul without any virtue, except a vulgar honesty, and he presents himself to receive the blessing of God. One receives the grace of the sacrament, but the other?

---

officium naturæ humanæ; sacramentum autem secundum quod est in institutione divina. Ergo sacramentum est principalius in matrimonio quam alia duo .... perfectio gratiæ est dignior perfectione naturæ.... fides et proles pertinent ad usum matrimonii, ... sed indivisibilitas, quam sacramentum importat, pertinet ad ipsum matrimonium secundum se .... et secundum hoc sacramentum est essentialius matrimonio quam fides et proles.—*Summ. Theol.*, supp., quæst. 49, a. 3.

[1] Conference I., The Sanctity of Marriage, part ii.

—And these marriages are made every day! Poor young girls know not how to resist the pressure of what are called human conventionalities. Deceived by the vague promises of an ill-regulated sentimentalism, they resign themselves to these kinds of mixed marriages, which ally their faith with indifference or incredulity, imagining that by strength of love they will subdue a rebellious heart to the grace of God. But they do not wait long for the chastisement of having lent their concurrence to the profanation of a sacrament, and they soon perceive that their marriage has failed.

It is a sad union, because God is not in it. They can forget this absence of God in the distractions of novelty and in the intoxication of their young love. But little by little the tie is loosened, preoccupations and trials begin to disturb life, and they find around them no common support, no refuge where two afflicted hearts can together find consolation. The only intimacy which time respects, religious intimacy, is impossible. They each retire sorrowfully into themselves, and an incurable sadness darkens the lives of those who counted on a cloudless future.

Such a union is sad and cruel. May not the Christian wife be struck with terror at the thought that she is, as it were, cursed in the half of her life; that God, Who inclines towards her, repulses him whom she loves best in the world; that there is a heartrending contradiction, almost a lie, in the promises by which two hearts that love have given themselves to each other, because they cannot be united in the noblest and most sacred portion of their life?

Sad and cruel, the union is also full of peril. Without faith and without the love of God, will a man employ against the religion of his wife the disloyal weapons of blasphemy and raillery? Will he carry on an impious war against her convictions and her religious practices, after having promised her liberty? Perhaps it may be so. But it is by the allurements of his love that man most easily assures the triumph of his irreligion. He knows how to appear so good, so tender, so full of natural virtue and amiable qualities, that the unfortunate companion of his life forgets that he is without grace, yields in cowardly compliance, and slips little by little down the slopes of a contemptible apostasy.

If the Christian woman, jealous of her liberty and faithful to her duty, resists violence and allurements of her infidel husband, she is condemned to a daily martyrdom. She understands then that she has no right to complain, but that she must repent of her errors and ask from the grace of God strength to be heroic. Who knows but that by her prayers, by her tears, by the sufferings of her martyred heart, she may perhaps obtain the conversion of her beloved, and enjoy with him some happy days in the winter of a union all the seasons of which have been desolate?

If such are the marriages in which the sacrament is only partly profaned, what must it be when the profanation is complete! Unfortunately, this crime is of more frequent occurrence than is generally believed. Under the power of laws which separate the civil contract from the religious marriage, it is only too common to regard the sacrament as a formality, in good taste, which might, strictly speaking, be done without, but which must still be submitted to, for fear of losing one's position in society. It is prepared for like a festival, which gives to the wedding more importance than the prosaic appearance of the affianced pair with their witnesses before a civil magistrate, the Pontiff of the State. They think of all the details of the festival, calculate the cost, invite relations and friends, and enjoy beforehand the splendor they desire to give to it. One thing only is forgotten, that it is an occasion for receiving the grace of God. After having extorted at the last moment an absolution which is useless, they go to kneel at the altar. And behold, there, at the invitation of the priest who is the witness of their vows, two sacrilegious ministers exchange between them a sacred thing of which neither of them can receive the full efficacy. Their word is sufficiently strong to impose on them a yoke, but not strong enough to adorn this yoke with the divine grace which would make it easy and light. Instead of grace, it is the divine curse which descends into the souls of these profaners, condemned to carry until the death of the one or the other the chain which the sacrilegious exchange of their vows has just forged.

Even when their union had been prepared for with all the precautions of human wisdom, it will be miserable, because grace is not there to correct the imperfections, the faults, and the vices of nature. How much the more if the union is tarnished with the iniquities and follies which dishonor the greater number of modern marriages! Expect all manner of evils, as the curse of God follows and chastises the sacrilege so long as reparation is not made. The two slaves of indissolubility will complain bitterly of being riveted to each other: so much the worse for them, their punishment is just. It is here that must be applied in all its divine severity this sentence of Wisdom: "By what things a man sinneth, by the same also he is tormented!" *Per quæ peccat quis, per hæc et torquetur.*[1]

There only remains to draw the conclusions from what you have just heard: they are self-evident. It is not the divine law which must be made responsible for the evils of which the adversaries of indissolubility complain. The divine law is wise because it is a law of progress and perfection; the divine law is just, because it chastises, according to their deserts, those who profane marriage. In pity for the innocent who sometimes suffer with the guilty, in pity for the guilty themselves, the Church consents to separations which, without breaking the conjugal tie, interrupt the living together and allow inconstant wills to be spared from committing irreparable faults, sick hearts to be healed far away from that which wounds them, repentance to come one day and

[1] Wis. xi. 17

knock at the door for pardon. It is all the Church can do. The divine law does not yield before misfortunes too often and too well merited. Far from being remedied, these misfortunes can only be aggravated by replacing the law of indissolubility with one of rupture and repudiation; divorce gives encouragement to folly and human perversity, and fatally multiplies the profanations whose lamentable consequences I have just explained to you. For the evils of marriage there is but one remedy, which is marriage itself, contracted with the conditions of self-respect, confidence in God, prudence, wisdom, disinterestedness, seriousness, sincerity, purity, a spirit of faith which will assure to husband and wife the possession of the three great blessings of their union.

Young men, listen to me. You must to-day understand that it is unjust to bring only a tarnished purity and an enfeebled life into a union in which you exact the integrity of virtue and the plenitude of life; that every immoral shaking of your senses is a terrible blow carried to your posterity; that large families have a special blessing from God; that children are the crown of their parents, the hope, the strength, the glory of your country. You must distrust that love which belongs only to the senses, regulate your choice, not after human custom, but according to Christian custom, remember that the choice is not obligatory and must be well considered, and that sincerity is the nearest allied to fidelity. Prepare for the sacrament with that religious respect which is due to sacred things, and with firm conviction that it alone is the true marriage.

In possession of the blessings which God promises to those who marry holily, piously bound with a chain which He has blessed and of which His unction softens the rigor, happy dwellers at a hearth where there is love, where religion is resplendent, where the peace of God reigns, you will prove to the world better than sermons, books, or treatises, that marriage, with its stern duties and its graces, is a great sacrament: *Sacramentum hoc magnum est.*

It is always great, always holy, even for those who have profaned it. By stopping the effusion of grace, they have in no way dried up its source; for this source is the very tie which unites them. Instead of complaining of its rigor and wearying themselves with vain efforts to break it, let them repent of their sacrilegious folly. The pardon of God can reopen the source which they have closed, and grace can yet sanctify the latter days of a union which has been unhappy only through the fault of those who contracted it without foreseeing its burdens and without due preparation for fulfilling its duties.

Conference VI.

Celibacy and Virginity.

My Lord[1] and Gentlemen:—The first and principal end of marriage is the propagation of the human race. God declared His designs in this respect by the commandment He gave to our first parents: "Increase and multiply, and fill the earth:" *Crescite, multiplicamini, et replete terram.* How would this law have worked in a state of innocence and immortality? We do not know, and there is no need of our knowing. Let us be content to learn from St. Thomas that it is unreasonable to believe with certain teachers that God, out of respect for the purity of our first parents, would have renewed in each member of humanity the great act of creation. In every state of existence it is an honor to give life and thus resemble the Principle of all life. In the state of innocence this honor would have been without peril and without stain. If our first parents had not sinned, they would have seen in the flesh the beauty with which God originally adorned it. Their upright nature, ignorant of the rebelliousness of the flesh, would have multiplied at the same time grace and life. In our fallen nature it is no longer thus. The honor of parentage remains, but it is accompanied

---

[1] Monseigneur Richard, Archbishop of Paris.

with so many inconveniences and dangers that one asks whether it is allowable to renounce it. Never, reply certain interpreters, too fervent and perhaps too interested in the law of population. This law is obligatory on all human beings. It is a reproach not to be able to fulfil it ; it is a crime voluntarily to withdraw from it. With such reasoning, we must acknowledge that God has shown Himself very prodigal in reproaches of our poor race, and that there is in Christian humanity a number of very interesting and perfect criminals.

It is of these last that I am about to speak to you, not to excuse, but to defend them. Against the general pretensions of the advocates of marriage at all costs, I wish to prove that celibacy and virginity may become a condition of choice: first, because this condition is desired by God; secondly, because it is one of the most beautiful and most useful ornaments of Christian society.

I.

We have seen God acting progressively in the institution of marriage. His will is manifested in the typical nuptials of our first parents; nevertheless, it is not yet expressly, imperatively, and definitely established, so as to forbid it every kind of indulgence towards the imperfections and failings of nature. The indissoluble unity of marriage is decreed, but God dispenses with it for reasons worthy of His infinite wisdom and His compassionate kindness. But His toleration does not make Him forget His original design, and to hinder the infirmity and perversity of man from prescribing against the unity and indissolubility of marriage, which He desires to be definitely established, He causes to be heard in the facts of history and in the teaching of Scripture protestations which bear witness to His preferences and show to which side the law of nature inclines. These protestations, we have seen, converge in a formal declaration by Christ, Who by virtue of His rights as Creator, Redeemer, Reformer, and Exemplar, brings back marriage to its primitive institution, and decrees for regenerate humanity the indispensable unity and indissolubility of the conjugal tie: *Et erunt duo in carne una.—Quod Deus conjunxit homo non separet.*[1] This slow and progressive march of God in the determination of the matrimonial law is remarked in the preparation of the evangelical counsel which requires of certain privileged souls a state nobler and more perfect than that of marriage. God desires this state, but before solemnly declaring His will He allows the human race to form this common opinion of celibacy and virginity which a great thinker voices in these words: "that it belongs to all ages, all places, all religions, and it sees in continence something celestial, which exalts man and renders him pleasing to the Divinity."[2] If the Jewish people, infatuated and proud of the oracles which promise it a deliverer born of its blood, esteems marriage above all other states, and regards sterility as a reproach, it never-

---

[1] Conference II., The Conjugal Tie, part i.
[2] Joseph de Maistre: *The Pope*, book iii., chap. 3.

theless demands continence from its priests at the periods when their sacred functions bring them into intercourse with God. It admires the holy reserve of women who in a way shroud themselves in their widowhood. Because you have loved chastity, said the High Priest Joachim to Judith, because you have not taken another husband, the hand of the Lord has strengthened you, you shall be blessed forever.[1]

The heathen themselves recognize the beauty of a state which protests against the corruption of their manners. They praise by the mouth of their poets and orators "the priests who always keep their chastity."[2] They call celibacy and virginity into the service of gods and goddesses. Isis, Minerva, Ceres, Vesta, are surrounded by virgins.[3] Virgins alone are worthy to watch the sacred fire and to receive the oracles of heaven;[4] virgins are venerable and holy.[4] Virgins deserve the greatest honors; the fasces bow before them; the first places are reserved for them at all the festivals where the majesty of the Senate and the Roman

[1] Eo quod castitatem amaveris, et post virum tuum alterum nescieris: ideo et manus Domini confortavit te, et ideo eris benedicta in æternum.—Judith xv. 11.
[2] Quique sacerdotes casti, dum vita manebat.—Virg. *Æneid* vi. 661.
[3] See the work of Joseph de Maistre, already cited.
[4] In the temple of Minerva at Athens the sacred fire was kept, as at Rome, by virgins. The same vestals are found among other nations, especially in India and Peru, and it is remarkable that the violation of their vow received the same punishment as at Rome.—Carli, *Lettere Americane*.
[5] (Numa) Virginitate aliisque cæremoniis venerabiles ac sanctas fecit.—Tit. Liv. i. 29.

people is displayed; and it is not too great a punishment to bury them alive if they have violated their oaths of chastity. Finally, it is in the womb of virgins and without the concurrence of man that the Theophani and divine avatars are formed.[1]

What a strange mystery is this in the traditions of heathenism! Is it an echo of the oracles announcing that the Virgin of virgins should bring forth Emmanuel? Is it the mystic dream of religious instinct in search of the state most suitable for the visits of Divinity? It matters little. I desire to see in it only the marvellous work of Providence, preparing in the ancient world the declaration of the divine desire which shall one day invite souls to a marriage far otherwise great and fecund than that of flesh and blood.

At the hour when the oracles of the sibyl virgins coincide with the celebrated prophecies of Isaias and Jeremias " the Lord hath created a new thing upon the earth:" *Creavit Dominus novum su-*

---

[1] The books of the Brahmins declare that when God deigns to visit the world, He becomes incarnate in the womb of a virgin without intercourse of sexes.—W. Jones, *Supp.* vol. ii., p. 548.

According to the Japanese, their great God Xaca was born of a virgin who never had intercourse with any man.—*Life of St. Francis Xavier*, by Father Bouhours, ii., liv. v.

The Maceniquians, a people in Paraguay, related to missionaries that a virgin of singular beauty had brought into the world a very beautiful child, which arrived at manhood, worked numerous miracles before his disciples, and transformed himself into the sun which we see.—Muratori, *Cristianesimo felice*, vol. i.

The Chinese generalize this doctrine. According to them, saints, wise men, deliverers are born of a virgin.—*Memoirs of Missionaries*, P. Cibot, vol. xi.

per terram. "A woman shall compass a man: " *Fœmina circumdabit virum.*[1] "Hear ye therefore, O house of David. ... Behold a virgin shall conceive and bear a son, and his name shall be called Emmanuel."[2] Virginity gives the Son of God to the world; the virginity of Mary and the celibacy of Joseph watch over His cradle, protect His infancy, and are admitted by a special privilege to contemplate the beauty of His great soul and the splendor of the eternal wisdom which radiate through the mysteries of His hidden life.

God is with us, virgin born of a virgin; in private He satisfies her with the vision of celestial things, and scarcely entered on His public life He promises this vision to those who are clean of heart:[3] *Beati mundo corde quoniam ipsi Deum videbunt.* And who, then, shall be clean of heart, if not those who voluntarily and forever separate themselves from the permitted pleasures of the flesh? The virgin Christ has no commandment for these as for those who marry; but at the very hour when He determines and fixes the legislation of marriage, He makes known His desire to draw them to Himself, and assigns them a special place in His kingdom. When His disciples, terrified at the rigor of the New Law, which suppresses the dispensations of the Old, and establishes the conjugal tie even until death, ask of Him if it were not

[1] Jerem. xxxi. 22.
[2] Audite, domus David. ... Dabit Dominus ipse vobis signum. Ecce virgo concipiet et pariet filium, et vocabitur nomen ejus Emmanuel.—Is. vii. 14.
[3] St. Matt. v. 8.

better to abstain from marriage, Jesus said to them: "All men take not this word, but they to whom it is given. For there are eunuchs who were born so from their mother's womb; and there are eunuchs who were made so by men, and there are eunuchs who have made themselves eunuchs for the kingdom of heaven. He that can take let him take it." Herein is a mystery.[1]

Yes, gentlemen, there is a mystery. And it is sufficient to make us understand that virginity is a state of choice and privilege, which no law commands and which corresponds to a most intimate and delicate desire of the most pure and most holy God, Who wills to form certain souls more nearly to His own perfection.

This desire is only once expressed by the Saviour. He reverts to it no more; He waits that His Spirit, poured out upon all flesh, may make the gift of God penetrate into souls. Then the great Paul is charged to remind the children of redemption of the counsel of the divine Master, to Whom he has consecrated the love of his heart and the integrity of his flesh.

The Apostle writes to the Corinthians: Brethren, ye are no more your own, for ye are bought with a great price. Glorify and bear God in your body. In reply to your inquiries, I tell you that it is good for a man not to touch a woman.... I

---

[1] Non omnes capiunt illud sed quibus datum est. Sunt enim eunuchi qui de matris utero sic nati sunt; et sunt eunuchi qui facti sunt ab hominibus; et sunt eunuchi qui seipsos castraverunt propter regnum cœlorum. Qui potest capere capiat.—St. Matt. xix. 11, 12.

would that all men were even as myself; but every one hath his proper gift from God, one after this manner and another after that.... Let every man wherein he was called, therein abide with God. It is true that I have received no commandment from the Lord touching virgins; but I give them this counsel, I who have obtained mercy of God to be faithful. It is good to be in this state. They who marry do not sin, but they are exposed to tribulations which I would spare you. He who has no wife thinks of God and seeks to please Him; he who is married is occupied with the things of the world and desires to please his wife: his heart is divided. The virgin thinks of the things of God, that she may be holy in body and spirit; she that is married thinks of the things of the world, how she may please her husband. I speak this for your profit, that ye may wait upon the Lord without distraction. Again, he who giveth his daughter in marriage doeth well, but he that giveth her not in marriage doeth better.... She shall be happier thus. This is what the Spirit of God has revealed to me.[1]

[1] Empti enim estis pretio magno. Glorificate et portate Deum in corpore vestro. De quibus autem scripsisti mihi: Bonum est homini mulierem non tangere.... Volo enim omnes vos esse sicut meipsum: sed unusquisque proprium donum habet ex Deo: alius quidem sic, alius vero sic.... Unusquisque in quo vocatus est, fratres, in hoc permaneat apud Deum. De virginibus autem præceptum Domini non habeo: consilium autem do, tamquam misericordiam consecutus a Domino, ut sim fidelis. .. Si acceperis uxorem, non peccasti; et si nupserit virgo, non peccavit; tribulationem tamen carnis habebunt hujusmodi. Ego autem vobis parco.... Volo autem vos sine solicitudine esse. Qui sine uxore est, solicitus est quæ Domini sunt, quomodo placeat Deo. Qui autem cum uxore est, solicitus est quæ sunt mun-

You will remark, gentlemen, that the Apostle, in order to encourage celibacy and virginity, speaks continually of the tribulations and cares of this life. Another virgin, the Apostle St. John, opens the doors of heaven and shows us around the Lamb thousands of enraptured choristers who make the holy mountain of Sion resound with a new song which no one can repeat after them. Those are they who have not tasted the dangerous sweets of terrestrial love: they are virgins. They have the privilege of following the Lamb wherever He goeth. Glorious first fruits of humanity, God has bought them for Himself and for the Lamb.[1]

You see, gentlemen, God does not command, He expresses a desire, He shows heaven. It is sufficient to determine and fix the choice of those who desire by the chastity of the body to honor the most pure flesh of Christ.[2] The first apostles

---

di, quomodo placeat uxori, et divisus est. Et mulier innupta, et virgo cogitat quæ Domini sunt, ut sit sancta corpore et spiritu ; quæ autem nupta est, cogitat quæ sunt mundi, quomodo placeat viro. Porro hoc ad utilitatem vestram dico, ...ad id quod honestum est, et quod facultatem præbeat sine impedimento Dominum obsecrandi. . . . Igitur et qui matrimonio jungit virginem suam, bene facit : et qui non jungit, melius facit. . . . Beatior erit si sic permanserit, secundum meum consilium: puto autem quod et ego Spiritum Dei habeam.—1. Cor. vi. 20; vii. 1, 7, 24, 25, 28, 32-35, 38, 40.

[1] Et vidi, et ecce Agnus stabat supra montem Sion et cum eo centum quadraginta quatuor millia. . . . Et cantabant quasi canticum novum, ... et nemo poterat dicere canticum. Illi sunt qui cum mulieribus non sunt coinquinati, virgines enim sunt. Hi sequuntur Agnum quocumque ierit. Hi empti sunt ex hominibus primitiæ Deo et Agno.—Apoc. xiv. 1, 3, 4.

[2] Si quis potest in casti ate ad honorem carnis Christi, in humilitate maneat.—S. Ignat. *ad Polycarp.*, vol. ii.

had scarcely closed their eyes when all conditions of Christian society were overspread by the luxurious growth of virgins who desired to live only for God. The holy Doctors show with legitimate pride to the infamous world, which has corrupted marriage, these parterres of living lilies, whose perfume God is pleased to inhale.[1]

Tertullian, Ambrose, Augustine, Jerome, Chrysostom, in sublime letters or learned treatises defend virginity against the slanders of heresy; they counsel and encourage chaste souls who have renounced the espousals of earth, whilst the inspired lyre of Gregory Nazianzen sings their praises, and asks for them from God the crowns which He cannot grant to the married ones of earth.[2] It may perhaps be objected to these defenders, these admirers of virginity, that they have treated marriage too severely, and therefore have exaggerated the desire of God; but for us there is an authority which brings it back to its just proportions, the authority of the Church.

On the one hand, the Church has proclaimed the sanctity of marriage and has covered it with the protection of her strong and wise legislation;

---

[1] Among us a great number of persons of both sexes, from sixty to seventy years of age, who from their childhood have been instructed in the doctrine of Jesus Christ, persevere in chastity, and I am constrained to show them in every condition of society.—S. Justin., *Apol.* i. 15.

There are among us a great number of men and women who live in celibacy, with the hope of being more closely united to God.—Athenagor., *Legatio pro Christianis*, n. 3.

[2] *Carmen in Laudem Virginitatis.*

on the other, she has not concealed at any time her preference for celibacy and virginity. She has desired that her priests should be those who receive the gift of God and spiritually mutilate themselves for the kingdom of heaven's sake. She has stretched out her arms to chaste souls, and has offered them a privileged place in her maternal heart. After the priesthood, virgins, with her, have a right to the greatest honors and to the tenderest solicitude of her love. She has withdrawn them from the world, where the purity of their life might be contaminated by scandalous spectacles and dangerous associations. She has built for them vast and beautiful dwellings, sometimes like palaces; angelic sanctuaries in whose favor she interests the faithful; of which she guards the door, armed with her censures and anathemas; where she regulates with jealous care all the details of a life entirely consecrated to God. There one enters only to marry the Eternal Bridegroom; these divine nuptials are a feast embellished with the most touching ceremonies and the sweetest chants of the Liturgy, and the Bishop, the father of the priesthood, alone has a right to bless them.

How beautiful, after fifteen centuries of Christianity, in the whole Catholic world is the glory of virginity! Around the enclosed gardens of the Bridegroom, Who delights in the midst of roses and lilies, heresy is silent, and marriage, honored with the blessing of God, acknowledges itself vanquished by the nobleness and the graces of a state where man renounces the consolations and joys of terrestrial love, in order to belong only to God.

But all of a sudden the impious outcry of the flesh is heard. Protestantism, in the name of God and in the name of nature, demands universal marriage. A libertine monk wants to excuse his apostasy; he can do it only by depreciating a state to which he has bound himself with an oath. "Away," says he, "with what is called evangelical counsel; we honor only the law. Now, the law to which those should submit who have sufficient life to give is the law of multiplication promulgated by the Creator: *Crescite, multiplicamini.* No one has understood the mysterious words of Christ, nor rightly seized the meaning of the Apostle; and the stupid admiration of the early centuries for a state which contradicts the will of God and outrages nature can only be the effect of a most pernicious fanaticism."

I need not remark to you, gentlemen, that this interested argument had for its aim to recruit around Luther imitators and companions of his treason. Priest and unfaithful religious, he wished to be able to say to other priests and other religious:—Let us marry, my brethren. They married, but they did not change the ordinance of perfection. The Church, tranquil in the midst of this matrimonial tempest, was content to inscribe in the chapter of her doctrine the expression of her profound esteem for a state which she knows to be desired by God. "If any one," she says, "maintains that the conjugal state should be preferred to virginity and celibacy, and that it is not better and happier to remain a virgin than to marry, let him be anathema."[1] And you will see that the Church is right.

II.

Man, the master of the earth, is obliged to cultivate it. He goes forth, says the Psalmist, to his work and remaineth till the evening: *Exibit homo ad opus suum et ad operationem suam usque ad vesperum.*[2] Under his diligent and courageous hand the furrows open and receive the fertile sowing, which shall come forth in the spring, and which, multiplied a hundredfold and gilded with the fire of the sun, shall be heaped up in the garners of the father of the family. Man has his duties. Who, then, shall contest his right to reserve for himself in his domain and near his dwelling a corner of earth less vulgar than the fertile plain; where bowers and parterres, verdure and flowers, rejoice his eye and waft him waves of perfume to rest his weariness and thank him for his labors? Now, God is a much greater lord than man. He has given man the earth, but humanity remains His domain, a domain of which the culture has increased, since Christ, by the effusion of His blood, has asserted His right over it as Redeemer. In the vast field of regenerated humanity the law of reproduction must be fulfilled. God works there every day, and to obtain a more abundant and

---

[1] Si quis dixerit statum conjugalem anteponendum esse statui virginitatis vel cœlibatus, et non esse melius ac beatius manere in virginitate aut cœlibatu, quam jungi matrimonio: anathema sit.—Conc. Trid., sess. 24, can. 10.

[2] Psalm ciii. 23.

more pure harvest of the offspring of human life, He has sanctified, as you have seen, the union between man and woman. Has he not a right, like the mere man who is a master, to reserve certain portions of his domain? And if there is a condition of life which draws man nearer to His holy majesty and assures Him more perfect homage, shall we be astonished if He desires and is pleased with it? And if it is true that He desires and is pleased with it, must we not behold in it one of the most beautiful ornaments of Christian society?

This state of life exists, gentlemen, the Church has just shown it to you; it is the state of celibacy and of virginity.

Understand me well. There is a shameful celibacy, which I deliver up to your contempt and to the malediction of economists who claim fecund lives for society; it is the celibacy of cowards, to whom marriage is only repugnant because they wish to avoid its duties and burdens in order to be freer for enjoyment. Reproach and cancer of society, Rome of old chastised it with the avenging laws which relegated it to the lowest places at the public games, lessened the authority of its votes in the Senate, deprived it of all testamentary inheritance, confiscated the legacies made in its favor, and assigned to married relatives its share of inheritances. Nothing could discourage it; helped by divorce, it accelerated the fall of the empire. This, no doubt, is what it prepares for modern society. But am I not wrong in calling that celibacy which is, after all, but selfish licentiousness?

It is not generally cold and idle chastity which refuses marriage, but it is the inexcusable immorality of those wretches who profess to multiply and vary their pleasures without wearing chains. If they abstain by chance from troubling families, or from seducing virtue, they do not fail to publish their scandalous alliances, until, wearied with adventures, exhausted with debauchery, they fall under the yoke of some servant-woman, who will pay with her utmost compliance for the inheritance she covets. Since human laws dare not touch these eunuchs of vice, let them be crushed by your contempt; they well deserve it.

Together with shameful celibacy, I give up to you that morose virginity which neither pardons nature for having ill-favored it, nor fortune for having refused it its bounties, nor the world for having condemned it, by its indifference or its scorn, to perpetual solitude. Sad heritage of decayed old maids, whose eager desires for matrimony change with age into malicious regrets. In their unspotted bodies their soured souls only think of revenging on all beauty, all virtue, all happiness, the forced celibacy which they consider a reproach. Eager manufacturers of slander, they give no rest to their venomous tongues when it is a question of injuring the best reputations. Flowers without perfume, lamps without oil, God, Who has not desired them, has promised to say to them one day: "I know you not:" *Nescio vos.*[1]

The virgins whom God desires, whom He knows

[1] St. Matt. xxv. 12.

and loves, are those whom He has touched with His grace, and who, responding to His loving advances by a free choice, have become copies of His perfection, angels of earth, the spouses of Christ, the living Gospel.

You ask me how voluntary sterility can be a copy of the perfection of God. The life of God is infinitely fecund. From Him all beings come forth, and in the mystery of His essence He gives Himself ineffable family joy, without multiplying His nature. They are three: the Father, the Son, and the Holy Ghost, and these three are one—eternal fecundity, which can neither do without nor weary of producing; inherent fecundity, which keeps its fruit within itself. All that is true, but the fecundity of God is so pure that no created fecundity can represent it. I said to you lately, when chanting the wonders of the divine procession: "The immaculate life of God derives from itself the power of propagating itself; nothing helps it, nothing fades it; it conceives without movement, it brings forth without labor, it loves without trouble; its tranquil procession perfects its beatitude without affecting its repose; according to the words of St. Gregory Nazianzen, it is the most beautiful and the first of virgins: *Prima virgo est sancta Trinitas*." [1]

Who can reproduce here below this chaste mystery?—The most charming flowers of humanity, like the most charming flowers of the field, cannot bear fruit without losing their virginity. One

---

[1] *Carmen in Laudem Virginitatis*, i., v. 20.

only creature in all time is called "the mother most admirable" and "the virgin most pure." But God has only once performed this miracle. In the rest of humanity, He has, as it were, divided in two the copies of His perfection. To some He has given the honor of representing His fecundity, to others the honor of representing His adorable purity. If those who bear children are proud to say, "God is father," those who renounce terrestrial marriages, so as to keep inviolate the treasure of their chastity, may also be proud to say, "God is virgin; the Holy Trinity is the first of virgins:" *Prima virgo est sancta Trinitas.*

Yes, gentlemen, God is virgin, and to virgins He reserves a more profound vision of His essence and of His life, and from virgins He expects a more perfect praise of His infinite beauty. The resplendent spirits next His throne are virgins. Their pure essences are not allied among themselves to multiply life, but they altogether are satisfied with the contemplation of the Word, the fruit of the life of God, and receive an immensity of light from the Holy Trinity, Whose purity they imitate! How far removed from these pure spirits are those whose faded flesh enchains the soul with the cares of this present life! Heaven is not refused to them, but they reach it only by slow steps, like that crawling animal which carries with it the weight of its house. Virginity, on the contrary, has wings which bear it towards the celestial regions, where the soul, free and mistress of itself, imitates the life of the angels.

It appears that the heathen themselves had some idea of this wonder. One of them, expressing the thought of a celebrated lawyer, said these remarkable words: "Celibacy and a spiritual man mean one and the same thing. Marriage divides a man by scattering him; continence gathers him up and brings him back to unity."[1] After the divine life there is nothing more one than the angelic life; after the angelic life there is nothing more one than the virginal life. In this life, the indivisible soul draws towards itself the divisible flesh, as if to shape it to its chaste simplicity, in order to remain fixed in contemplation, in love, and in the worship of divine things. Freed by chastity from the appetites and desires of the flesh, the soul, says St. Thomas, is better disposed for intellectual work.[2] The absence of corruption enables it to live close to incorruptibility: *Incorruptio facit esse proximum Deo;*[3] and God promises to it the vision of divine mysteries: *Beati mundo corde, quoniam ipsi Deum videbunt.*[4]

The virginal soul, in fact, sees God everywhere; not only in eternal principles, which appear more clear to it, through the luminous transparency which chastity gives to them; not only in the principles of faith, upon which it can meditate at leis-

---

[1] Cajus cœlibes dixit quasi cœlites et cœlestes, quod onere gravissimo vacent nuptiarum; per continentiam quippe colligimur et redigimur in unum, a quo in multa defluximus.—*Quintilian*, lib. i., cap. x.

[2] Castitas maxime disponit ad perfectionem operationis intellectualis.—*Summ. Theol.*, I. II. P. quæst. 15, a. 3.

[3] Wis. vi. 20.

[4] St. Matt. v. 8.

ure; but in all creatures, who have no other charm in its eyes, purified from all earthly covetousness, except that they represent the infinite perfections of the Creator. More rejoiced than others by the vision of God, the virginal soul feels more captivated with a greater love for Him; and this love, freed from the attachments, preoccupations, and troubles of life, which entangle, vulgarize, and weigh down conjugal life, is always ready to burst forth into praises. To see, to love, to praise God, is not that the angelical life? This was necessary for our human world since a God has visited it. "When the Son of God came on earth," writes St. Jerome to his dear virgin Eustochia, "He made for Himself a special family; and as He had angels for adorers in heaven, He wished also to have angels for servants here below."[1]

Better still. The virgins who have despised the alliance of men should have in Christian society a still higher destiny than to serve the God Whose angels they are. At least their service is elevated by an august title which opens to them the gates of the mysterious regions of the spiritual life in which God makes Himself intimately known. The virgin serves Christ with the title of the privileged spouse. "The King of kings," says the Church, "hath desired her beauty:" *Concupiscet rex decorem tuum.*[2] She on her part, insensible

---

[1] Statim ut Filius Dei ingressus est super terram novam sibi familiam instituit, ut qui ab angelis adorabatur in cœlo, haberet angelos et in terris.—Epist. xi. *ad Eustochiam.*

[2] Ps. xliv. 12.

to the attractions of creatures, has better understood the charms of the God humiliated, Who has sought her. They have met in solitary and quiet regions, where no noise of earth is heard. And Christ has said: *Veni, electa mea:* "Come My chosen one!" And the virgin has exclaimed: "I have despised the world and the vain ornaments of the age for the love of my Master, Jesus Christ. I have seen Him, I have loved Him, I have confidence in Him, I have chosen Him for my heritage."[1] The union is complete.

Nuptials of the flesh, how insignificant you are beside these spiritual nuptials! Here, also, there are vows. The virgin, in receiving the sacred veil, protests her humble and sincere submission to the divine Spouse Whom she has chosen.[2] Married to the Eternal Bridegroom, she cannot break her vow without becoming an adulteress, and worthy of eternal death: *Adulterium perpetrat et ancilla mortis efficitur.*[3] But in exchange for her fidelity, the Celestial Spouse covers her with His protection, lavishes on her His graces, and reserves for her the intimate confidences of His love. Thanks to these confidences, she knows secrets

---

[1] Regnum mundi et omnem ornatum sæculi contempsi, propter amorem Domini mei Jesu Christi, quem vidi, quem amavi, in quem credidi, quem dilexi.—*Response in the Office of Virgins.*

[2] Accipe velamen sacrum, quo cognoscaris mundum contempsisse, et te Christo Jesu veraciter humiliterque toto corde sponsam in perpetuum subdidisse.

[3] Quæ se spopondit Christo, et sanctum velamen accepit, jam nupsit, jam immortali juncta est viro, et jam si voluerit nubere communi lege, adulterium perpetrat, et ancilla mortis efficitur.—S. Ambrose, *ad virginem lapsam.*

which only the chaste soul can receive and understand of the perfections of God, of the mysteries of the faith, of the merit of virtue, of the progress of the spiritual life.

And now, gentlemen, behold the noble fruit of these divine nuptials: the virgin, the confidant of the intimate word of Christ, her spouse, becomes His exterior word, His living Gospel. Christ has spoken to the world, not only to reveal to it the mysteries which reason can neither know nor understand by its own power, but also to give it the measure of perfection to which human life can attain. The Gospel, with its precepts and counsels, is the code of this perfection.

It is not easily found among those who are entangled in the bonds of married life. The flesh and the spirit are at continual war with them, and it is a difficult task to make the subdued flesh walk in the way of the spirit. The Christian husband and wife must never lose sight of the dignity to which they have been raised by the grace of their spiritual birth and the infusion of the divine life. It is no easy task to keep within bounds, and much time is required to subject the tyranny of the senses to reason. When a married couple succeed in establishing the dominion of reason over the senses, they should try to disengage their hearts and repair the injustice they may have done to the holy love of God, which is too often forgotten in an earthly love.

Parents have to discharge the duties of a providence for their children. Too weak for this great function, they bend under the weight of the preoccupations and cares on which the existence and fate of the family depend, and they are no longer able to raise the standard of their spiritual life as high as they desire. Marriage is certainly an honorable and a holy state, because God has blessed it; but those who wish to live the married life of Christians must not conceal from themselves that perfection encounters a thousand obstacles, and that it is rare in it. It is doing much to walk uprightly in the ordinary way of the commandments.

Virginity, on the contrary, goes beyond precepts, and enters in the beginning through the special door of the evangelical counsels. And to protect as well as to expand it, it calls to its aid a number of virtues which render it more beautiful and charming. There happens in the virginal life something analogous to the physiological phenomenon remarked in those flowers which man makes sterile in order to increase their beauty. Here, culture transforms the organs of fecundity into sparkling petals and delicious perfume; there, under the influence of grace, all that chastity retrenches from the life of sense it adds to the development of virtue. These virtues are born, as it were spontaneously, from the reserves of divine grace which the chaste soul accumulates in an inviolate flesh. Humility, modesty, recollection, contempt of worldly goods, voluntary poverty, abnegation, obedience, mortification, group around virginity to defend it and to increase its splendor. Religion often strengthens these virtues by vows which make of the virginal life one perpetual holocaust. Briefly, the fulfilment of divine precepts is crowned in the state of celibacy and virginity by the practice of the evangelical counsels. This state is a radiant expression of that perfection taught by the Saviour; I have well called it His living Gospel.

After this, I am not astonished at the enthusiasm with which a pious admirer of this noble and holy state exclaims: "The life of the soul is as much above the life of the flesh as the immense heaven is above our narrow planet, as the stability of the blessed is above our fleeting existence; as God is above man, so is virginity above marriage."[1] Virginity, viewed in this light, you will agree with me, is one of the most beautiful ornaments of Christian society. To desire to suppress it for the benefit of what are called fecund lives, is,—pardon the comparison,—as if it were proposed to devastate around a magnificent palace the parterres, the lawns, and the bowers, in order to replace them by a field of potatoes, which could very well grow elsewhere.

Besides, you must not think virginity is a useless ornament in the world. There is more than one way of being useful, and the service of the multiplication of species can be largely compen-

Τοσσάτιον προφέρουσα γάμου βιότοιό τε δεσμῶν,
Ὁσσάτιον ψυχὴ προφερεστέρη ἔπλετο σαρκός,
Καὶ χθονὸς οὐρανὸς εὐρὺς, ὅσον βιότοιο ῥέοντος
Ἑστηὼς μακάρεσσιν, ὅσον Θεὸς ἀνδρὸς ἀρείων.
    S. Greg. Naz., *op. cit.*, v. 205–208.

sated in society by other domestic and public services. Time does not permit me to give to this interesting consideration all the development it would bear. I hope, however, to say sufficient to justify the definition of the Church and to complete the apology which I have undertaken. Let us confine ourselves to notice three great social benefits of virginity: the service of example, the service of prayer, the service of devotedness.

There is a terrible struggle in our fallen nature between the flesh and the spirit; it can only terminate to our honor by the triumph of the spirit. Now, this triumph is nowhere more complete than in the virginal life. Marriage is a concession made to the lower part of ourselves; virginity will grant nothing. "Heroic enterprise!" says the great Chrysostom, "I know the difficulties and violence of the combat, and the heavy burden of this warfare without truce and without mercy. It requires a courageous and strong soul, a heart full of aversion for voluptuousness. Dust and ashes, we have resolved to equal those who crowd yonder the celestial courts. It is mortality which enters into combat with immortality."[1] Sublime struggle, at the end of which virginity becomes the

---

[1] Οἶδα τὴν βίαν τοῦ πράγματος, οἶδα τῶν ἀγωνισμάτων τούτων τὸν τόνον, οἶδα τοῦ πολέμου τὸ βαρύ. Φιλονεικου τινὸς καὶ βιαίας καὶ ἀπονενοημένης κατὰ τῶν ἐπιθυμιῶν δεῖ ψυχῆς......'Η γῆ καὶ ὁ σποδὸς τοῖς ἐν οὐρανῷ διατρίβουσιν ἐξισοῦσθαι φιλονεικεῖ, καὶ ἡ φθορὰ πρὸς τὴν ἀφθαρσίαν τὴν ἅμιλλαν ἔθετο.—S. Chrys., *De Virginitate*, n. 27.

light of the world: *Virginitas est splendor.*[1] To those who endure the ardent conflicts of which the Apostle complains, it teaches that there is in the Christian soul sufficient strength and sufficient grace to discipline and to subdue the life of sense. In doing more than God exacts, it exalts the authority and wisdom of His commandments; and its example is, for cowardly souls, a living censure, for willing souls, a powerful inducement. Courage! it says to them; you shall have sufficient strength to regulate the pleasure which God permits, because I have severed myself from it forever. Believe me, it' is no small matter for a world tormented by passion to have constantly before its eyes the personification of. the triumph of the spirit over the flesh.

Virginity enters into the noble career of social service in a more active manner by prayer. Every reasonable creature is obliged to pray, the Christian more than any other. But, in order to obtain through this act a perfection which shall draw it nearer to His infinite majesty, God has desired that certain souls should make prayer their work and their profession. It is a way of lifting one's self up to Him, of contemplating His perfections, of speaking to Him, of laying bare to His infinite pity the miseries of nature, of moving Him to mercy and forcing Him to pacific contract with His creature; it is supereminently a state of the

---

[1] Conjugium est indulgentia libidini concessa; virginitas autem splendor: Γάμος συγγνώμη πάθους, ἁγνεία δὲ λαμπρότης.—S. Naz., Carm. III., *Exhortat. ad Virgines*, v. 20.

Christian soul in which is revealed so admirable an elevation of the spirit; such a deep tenderness of heart; such a power of remembrance, of sight, of sentiment, of expression, of accents unknown to the noblest and greatest arts; a state, in short, which places man so near God, God so near man, that it must be acknowledged to be the divine art *par excellence—ars divinior*. Now, the virgin possesses better than any one the secrets of this divine art, because, having chosen God for her portion, she sees Him nearer and lives in His intimacy. Besides, from the height of her life, freed from the solicitudes and tribulations of the age, she perceives what is wanting in the worship of God among the crowd of those whose homage He awaits; powerlessness, negligence, forgetfulness, proud determination to calculate only on human effort, all these religious disorders touch her deeply, and she feels the need of offering to her divine Spouse compensations drawn from her own life. She multiplies therefore the loving emotions of her heart and the chaste supplications of her lips, in order that society may always have the same number of benefits, because, thanks to her devotedness, God shall always have the same quantity of prayers.

I have just named devotedness, but you are not ignorant of that source of the most useful and most noble services that men can render to each other in social life. Every man, every Christian, is capable of devotedness. But the faculty of devoting one's self is for the most part limited, in the different conditions of life, by the duties which retain the heart beside those whom it loves, and prevent its casting itself blindly and without reason into the way of sacrifice. We are devoted to our own; but to forget our own, to be devoted to strangers, is more than human nature can do. I see self-sacrifice become illustrious from time to time by heroic acts; it cannot make a habit nor a profession of them. Virginity alone gives it this strange power. By renouncing earthly marriage, the virgin frees herself from the servitude of flesh and blood, and from those imperious family affections which gauge generosity of heart and impose on it certain reservations. All belongs to her, all within her is free. To all the unfortunate, to all miseries which ask for consolation and help, to all public misfortunes, to all the great causes for which sacrifice must be made, she is always ready to say: "Here I am:" *Ecce adsum.*

Now, gentlemen, you will understand better why the Church asks from her priests celibacy. For a chosen ministry, there must be a chosen state. The priest, invested with the highest of dignities, the official confidant of God and the minister of His grace, should belong entirely to Him. The less right the creature has to him, the more he is a man of God; the more he is a man of God, the more should he resemble the angels, whom Scripture calls the ministers of the Most High. Sacred captain of the Christian army, the more victories he can show, the more fitted is he to regulate the combat maintained against the passions of the flesh; and the absolute triumph of spirit in his virgin body speaks more eloquently than all sermons. Precentor of the Christian world, he requires all his time, all his attention, and all his heart to keep himself in communion with God. It is his office to immolate a divine victim, and no cares of married life must be allowed to interfere with that duty. Confidant of sinners, he receives their confessions more freely in a virginal soul whose secrets no intimate love fathoms. Minister of Providence, he is not tempted, if he is alone, to economize, from the share of the unfortunate, a patrimony for a family. Apostle of truth, he can carry it from day to day, from one place to another, and even to the ends of the earth, if he has no other care than changing only his own place of abode. Defender of a holy doctrine, he might yield to the threats of persecutors, to save the liberty and the life of the wife who should be one flesh with him, the children to whom he should have given his heart with his blood; virgin, he can say without hesitation to tyrants: Take my liberty, take my life; you shall not have my faith!

Understand, once again, why the Church lovingly cultivates virgins. They are the sacred tithe of her most pure possessions which she offers to Christ, her Spouse; they are the supreme resource of her heart desolated by human prevarications. God is much forgotten and grievously offended in the world, but at least the Church has raised in the state of virginity a holy mountain, a fertile mountain, a mountain where grace abounds, a mountain where God is pleased to dwell: *mons Dei, mons pinguis, mons coagulatus, mons in quo beneplacitum est Deo habitare in eo.*[1] From it He scatters the greater part of the gifts which He bestows on Christian society, to comfort it in the daily struggles between good and evil; from it ascends the perpetual *miserere* which stays the divine anger on its way. Without the compensations of virginal prayers social life would be continually harassed by the visitations of the justice of God.

But not only do virgins whom the Church loves and nurtures protect us from the justice of God, they are the most active and devoted instruments of His mercy. The ignorant, the insane, the orphan, the aged, the poor, the sick, the infirm, the incurable, find in them mothers, daughters, sisters, ever ready to render them the most delicate and the most loathsome service. Epidemics and contagious diseases attract them. They hasten to them with a free and joyous heart, for no despairing voice cries behind them: Do not go there;—and the voice of the Spouse Whom they have chosen, and Who is incarnate in the unfortunate, says to them: Come unto Me.

They are not all in convents, these sweet mothers of human miseries. They are in many families whom misfortune has visited. You have met them, and perhaps you have regarded them with disdainful compassion. You were to blame.

[1] Ps. lxvii.

All are not, as you think, victims disgraced by nature and by fortune. There are those who have had a glimpse of the joys of a happy union, and the sweets of the religious life : but they have immolated their hopes and their desires to consecrate themselves to the obscure tasks in which their life is consumed. I cannot better describe them than by copying a great writer who has personally witnessed their devotion.[1] "For the love of God, they have refused both the love of man and even the service of God; by charity, they have separated themselves from the joys of charity. They have not fully either the peace of the cloister, nor the care of the poor, nor apostleship in the world, and their great heart has known how to deprive itself of all that is great and perfect. They have enclosed their lives in little duties: supports of aged parents who load them with their exactions; servants of brothers and sisters afflicted in the loss of the dear one of their life; mothers of orphans, they replace the absent ones, whom selfishness or death has carried off, giving themselves entirely and receiving only in part. Youth, liberty, future, they have sacrificed all! Oh! widowed virgins, religious without veil, spouses without rights, mothers without the name, blessed are ye! The despising voice of the world calls you old maids, but you shall be proud and well avenged when, in presence of the whole world, Christ shall open to you His arms and shall say : *Veni sponsa mea :* Come, My spouse!"

[1] Louis Veuillot, *Çà et là.*

Such is virginity. If you have understood the grandeur of this holy state, you will not ask me to reply to the insipid considerations of economy and to the unjust recriminations of those who accuse virgins of diminishing social life, and of outraging nature.¹ For the rest, you will find in the apology you have just heard all the elements of a refutation, and if you will allow your good sense to speak, it will say to you with Gregory of Nazianzen: *Nobis fas non est probrum infundere virginitati;* "we are not permitted to cast opprobrium on virginity."²

But your Christian souls will not be satisfied with abstaining from outrage; with the Church they will sing this beautiful canticle of Wisdom: "O how beautiful is the chaste generation with glory: for the memory thereof is immortal: because it is known both with God and with men."³ But, also, marriage is only a condition of our passing life; virginity is an eternal state, like the purity of the angels, which it imitates in this world and in heaven. *Neque nubent, neque nubentur, sed erunt sicut angeli Dei in cœlo.*⁴

¹ Cf. Index at the end of the volume.
² ‘Ἡμῖν δ'οὐ θέμις ἐστὶν ἐλεγχείην καταχεύειν
    Παρθενίης. . . . . . .
S. Greg., Carm. II., *Præcepta ad Virgines*, v. 507-508.
³ O quam pulchra est casta generatio cum claritate! Immortalis est enim memoria illius: quoniam apud Deum nota est et apud homines.—Wis. iv. 1.
⁴ They shall neither marry nor be married: but shall be as angels of God in heaven.—St. Matt. xxii. 30.

INDEX

OF THE PRINCIPAL ERRORS CONTRARY TO THE
DOGMAS SET FORTH IN THIS VOLUME.

CONFERENCE I.

(*See the first part: Sanctity of marriage in the order of nature.*)

THE ancient heretics, Simon, Saturninus, the *Gnostics*, taught that marriage had not been instituted by God, and considered it a shameful thing. The *Manicheans*, according to their system, which attributed the creation of bodies to the evil spirit, maintained that the procreation of children was suggested by the demon, and only served to extend his empire. They thus condemned marriage as an absolutely bad institution.

"Man," said *Manes*, in his conference with Archelaus, Bishop of Charcar, "man cannot be the work of God, because intemperance, passion, and fornication preside over his generation." In Manicheism the elect or perfect renounced marriage. If they permitted it to the imperfect, it was with the counsel to hinder generation. The *Eustathians, Euchites, Priscillianists, Albigenses, Lollards*, offshoots of Manicheism, taught that marriage is only a sworn prostitution, to avoid which they gave themselves up to the most abominable promiscuousness.

The greater part of these heretics have been refuted by St. Irenæus, Clement of Alexandria, Tertullian, Origen, St. Epiphanius, St. Augustine, Theodoret, and other writers.

The Council of Gangra (341) condemns those who blame marriage and embrace virginity, not for the excellence of this virtue, but because they consider marriage evil. "We admire virginity," say the Fathers of the Council, "and also separation from the world, provided they are joined to modesty and humility; but we also respect marriage and desire that all that is conformable to Holy Scripture should be practised."

(*See the second part: The sacrament.*)

Protestantism does not deny the divine institution of marriage, but excludes it from the number of the sacraments. *Luther* saw in it neither a sacred sign nor the promise of grace (*Lib. de Captivitate Babylon:* cap. *De Matrimonio*). *Calvin* affirms that there is no more sacrament in marriage than in the practice of the most vulgar trades: *Non magis sacramenti ratio matrimonio convenit quam agriculturæ, aut tonstrinæ, aut sutoriæ arti* (Lib. iv. *Institut.*, cap. xix., § 34). *Melanchthon* and *Khemnitz* appear to have been attached to the opinion of *Durand*, who asserts that marriage cannot be strictly called a sacrament, but only in an equivocal manner. The theory of Durand is of small importance compared with the teaching of all theologians and the constant tradition of the Church.

Bergier makes this judicious remark with regard to the Protestant doctrine: "Since it has pleased the Protestants to decide that sacraments do not produce by themselves sanctifying grace in the souls of those who receive them, that all their effect consists in exacting faith, which alone justifies, we do not see why they exclude marriage from the number of the sacraments. Is this ceremony less fitted to excite faith in the faithful than Baptism or the Lord's Supper? The mutual promises which the married pair make of an inviolable fidelity, the blessing of the Church which consecrates these promises, should persuade them, no doubt, that God ratifies them, that He will give them the graces and the strength which they need to enable them to live holily, to aid and support each other, and to bring up their children in a Christian manner" (*Diction. theol.*, art. *Marriage*).

(*See ibid.: The minister of the sacrament.*)

We have considered the contracting parties in marriage as the ministers of the sacrament. It is the opinion to which to-day the theological schools return, because it is in fact the opinion of tradition.

A good number of theologians have deviated from this opinion, following *Melchior Cano*. They teach that the priest is the chief minister of the sacrament of marriage. The contracting parties only present the matter, which is their consent; the priest makes the sacrament by applying the form to the matter in these words: *Ego vos conjungo.* The principal arguments on which this opinion rests are:

1. In the New Testament, the words in which the Apostle St. Paul declares that the priests are the dispensers of the divine mysteries: *Sic nos existimet homo ut ministros Christi et dispensatores mysteriorum Dei* (I. Cor. vi. 1).

2. In tradition, the testimony of the Fathers, who require the sacerdotal benediction, and attribute to it the power of joining the married pair and of conferring grace. *Obsignat benedictio* (Tertul., *Ad uxor.* cap. viii.). *Cum ipsum conjugium velamine sacerdotali et benedictione sanctificare oporteat* (S. Ambrose, Epist. xix. *ad Vigilium*). *Jugum per benedictionem impositum sit distantium conjunctio* (S. Basil, in *Hexameron,* hom. vii.). *Quantum ad voluntatem attinet et adsum, et simul festum celebro juvenilesque dextras inter se jungo atque utrasque Dei manui* (S. Greg. Naz., Epist. lvii. *ad Procopium*), etc.

To the testimony of the Fathers is added the testimony of Councils; from the Third Lateran Council, which forbids priests to receive anything for blessing marriage and conferring the other sacraments (Cap. *Cum in Ecclesia,* ix. *de simonia*); from the Council of Florence, which declares that in all the sacraments of the New Law three things are necessary: the matter, the form, and the person of the minister conferring the sacrament: *Omnia sacramenta novæ legis tribus perficientur, videlicet, rebus tanquam materia verbis tanquam, forma, et persona ministri conferentis sacramentum.*

These arguments from authorities have little strength, and are easily refuted.

First, it is manifest that in the chapter where St. Paul calls the apostles dispensers of the mysteries of God, he desires to speak of the ministry of preaching. To apply this text to the administration of the sacraments, and to make use of it as an instrument of war to demolish a teaching of tradition, is to go beyond the intention of the Apostle, who, even had he intended indirectly to signify the sacraments, would then only have spoken of those whose administration is intrusted to the preachers of the Gospel.

As to the Fathers and Councils, if they recommend the nuptial benediction, it is evidently in order to protest against clandestine marriages, to arouse the piety of the faithful, and to give them a higher idea of the sacrament.

Tertullian, in his book, *Ad uxorem*, recommends the faithful to receive this benediction, so as to remove all suspicions of fornication and concubinage, which rest upon those who marry privately.

St. Ambrose, in his letter *A Virgile*, does not mention the benediction which, according to Cano, would be the form of the sacrament, but that which accompanies the placing the veil on the heads of the married pair; a benediction which is never given to a second marriage, which nevertheless is a sacrament.

St. Basil does not refer to the sacerdotal benediction, but to the benediction which God gave to our first parents.

In the text of St. Gregory Nazianzen, who excuses himself for not having been present at the marriage of Olympiade, it is evident that he speaks of a presence destined to give more solemnity to the marriage, and not of a benediction on which the validity of the sacrament depends. As to the decree of the Lateran Council against simony, it in no way assimilates marriage with the other sacraments as regards its sacerdotal administration. It speaks simply of the celebration of marriage as a sacred function for which money should not be demanded. If the argument of those who consider the priest as the minister of marriage were true in this instance, we should have to say that funeral services and burials, of which the Council speaks in the same decree, are sacraments. The text of the Council of Florence proves absolutely nothing in favor of the opinion of Cano. It requires the presence of a minister, but it does not say that this minister should be a priest. Besides, the doctrine of the Fathers of Florence on this point is manifestly expressed in the text where they say that the efficient cause of marriage is the consent of the contracting parties: *Causa efficiens matrimonii regulariter est mutuus consensus per verba de præsenti expressus.*

The opinion of Cano is more plausible on the side of theological arguments. It multiplies difficulties, but there are none which cannot be solved. These are the principal ones:

Firstly, everything in a sacrament should be sacred: the matter, the form, the ministry. Now, in the contract, all is secular; nothing distinguishes, as to its elements, that of Catholics from that of infidels.

Secondly, in the sacrament the precise and determined form should be applied to the matter: *Accedit verbum ad elementum et fit sacramentum.* Now, in the matrimonial contract, it is not easy to distinguish form from matter, and consent may be expressed in various ways, even by signs.

Thirdly, the Church sometimes permits marriages between Catholics and non-Catholics. But if the contracting parties are ministers, they commit a double sacrilege, the one in administering a sacrament to another who is unworthy; the other in fulfilling a sacred function of which he is incapable.

Fourthly and lastly, it is impossible that the Church should put into the mouths of her ministers words which mean nothing. But this is what would happen if the contracting parties were ministers. Their consent would unite them, and the words of the priest, *Ego vos in matrimonium conjungo*, would have absolutely no effect.

We reply to this:

Firstly, all becomes sacred in the contract the moment God raises it to the dignity of a sacrament conferring grace and representing the union between Christ and His Church.

Secondly, in the contract the matter is perfectly distinct from the form. The matter is the dona tion which one of the parties makes of itself, the form is the acceptation of this donation by the other party. It matters little that the donation and acceptation be expressed in different ways, and even by signs, provided that there is a veritable contract which God raises to the dignity of a sacrament.

Thirdly, when the Church permits a marriage between Catholic and non-Catholic, the latter receives the power to confer the sacrament on his or her partner, and for this it is sufficient that there should be the intention to do what the Church does. And, consequently, there is no sacrilege on the part of the non-Catholic. There is no more sacrilege on the side of the Catholic party, who, only wishing to do what the Church does, intends only to form the tie and not to give grace to one who is unable to receive it.

Fourthly, the words of the priest are not without signification in the celebration of marriage. They express the solemn approbation which the Church gives to a union contracted beneath her eyes.

Soon after Cano had put forth his opinion, a great number of theologians embraced it, among others, Sylvius, Estius, Juvenin, Piette, Gibert, Du Hamel, L'Herminier, Tournely; still, Tournely confesses that if number should decide the victory, the opinion of scholastics carries it: *Si ex auctoritate et numero scholasticorum pugnandum hic foret, vinceret haud dubio opposita sententia* (*Tract. de matrimonio*). But since this the number of the partisans of Melchior Cano has greatly increased, so that Roskovany dares to write that the number of modern theologians who maintain the opinion of the contracting parties being ministers is very few: *Ex recentioribus paucissimi veterum scholasticorum complectuntur opinionem, quasi scilicet ipsi contrahentes sacramentum matrimonii sibi administrarent."*

Benedict Stattler goes further and asserts that the Church can define dogmatically to-day this proposition: "The priest is the minister of the sacrament of marriage."

Stattler is mistaken. The Church will not define, the Church cannot define, an entirely new opinion, which is a manifest deviation from the teaching of the schools up to the time of the Council of Trent.

Cano understood so well the great importance and authority of this teaching that he endeavored to attach his opinion to that of some scholastics. But he passes over William de Paris and Peter de Palude (Paludanus); and St. Thomas, from whom he extracts a few doubtful texts, gives him a formal denial.

According to the holy Doctor, the benediction of the priest is not the essence of marriage. It is simply, like many other benedictions, a kind of sacramental: *Benedictio sacerdotis non est de essentia matrimonii, sed est quoddam sacramentale* (In. 4, *sent. dist.* 26, q. 1, a. 1 ad 2). And, besides, he affirms that the words by which the contracting parties express their consent directly make the conjugal tie, which is the sacrament of marriage: *Verba consensum experimentia directe faciunt nexum quemdam, qui est sacramentum matrimonii* (Ibid. a. 3 ad 3).

The authority of this teaching has great force for the opinion of those who consider the contracting parties as the ministers of the sacrament of marriage. The testimony of Scripture and of tradition does not fail them.

In the text where St. Paul compares the union of man and woman to the union of Christ and His Church, there is no question of the intervention of the priest nor of his blessing, and it is manifestly to the act by which the married pair give themselves to each other that the Apostle applies these words: *Sacramentum hoc magnum est.*

As to the Fathers, if we examine closely their testimony, we are convinced that they regard the blessing of the priest only as a ceremony necessary to the publicity and solemnity of the sacrament, and not to its essence.

Tertullian, for example, after having said that the blessing of the priest seals the union between husband and wife, adds: " There are among us unions which are not made before the Church, and they run the risk of being accused of adultery and fornication:" *Ideo penes nos occultæ quoque conjunctiones, hoc est non prius apud Ecclesiam professæ, juxta mœchiam et fornicationem judicari periclitantur* (Lib. ii., *ad uxorem*).

These words indicate plainly that the sacerdotal blessing is a measure of public honesty and nothing else: or else Tertullian would have simply said that clandestine unions are fornications.

It is proper, says St. Ignatius, the martyr, that husbands and wives *should make their union* with the consent of the bishop. It is, then, the husbands and wives who make the union, and the intervention of the priest is only a matter of propriety.

St. Augustine, in book i., *De Nuptiis et Concupiscentia*, explains the text of St. Paul in the sense we have indicated above: *Quod in Christo et in Ecclesia est magnum sacramentum, hoc est in singulis quibusque viris atque uxoribus minimum, sed tamen conjunctionis inseparabile sacramentum.*

But the strongest argument in favor of the contracting parties is assuredly the doctrine and practice of the Church. Now, the Council of Florence, after having said: *Septimum est sacramentum matrimonii*, adds: *Causa efficiens matrimonii regulariter est mutuus consensus per verba de præsenti expressus.* The Council of Trent, in the first chapter of the twenty-fourth session, declares that clandestine marriages are true marriages, having the character of sacraments, so long as the Church has not taken measures to invalidate them, and it says anathema to those who contradict this doctrine: *Tametsi dubitandum non est, clandestina matrimonia libero contrahentium consensu facta rata et vera esse matrimonia, quamdiu Ecclesia ea irrita non fecit ; et proinde jure damnandi sint illi, ut eos sancta synodus anathemate damnat qui ea vera ac rata esse negant.* . . . .

The sense of the word *rata*, which the Council of Trent employs, is clearly determined by Innocent III., *Decret.*, cap. *Quanto*. Comparing the marriage of Christians with that of infidels, this Pontiff calls the latter *verum et non ratum*, the former, *verum et ratum*, because it is a sacrament : *Nam etsi matrimonium* VERUM *inter infideles existat, non tamen est* RATUM *; inter fideles autem* VERUM *et* RATUM *existit ; quia sacramentum fidei, quod semel ut admissum, numquam amittitur sed* RATUM *efficit conjugii* SACRAMENTUM *ut ipsum in conjugibus illo durante perduret.*

In practice, clandestine marriages are considered true marriages everywhere where the Council of Trent has not been promulgated.

By exacting the presence of the priest, the Council has not claimed to appoint him minister of the sacrament, but as a witness commissioned by the Church to watch over a holy action. By introducing the obstacle of clandestinity, it has not denied the sacred power of the contracting parties, but it has rendered them incapable of contracting.

This argument appears to us irrefutable; it is the strongest that can be made in favor of the contracting parties being ministers.

It is incomprehensible how Stattler has dared to affirm that the Church was in a position to define this opinion dogmatically:—the priest is the minister of the sacrament of marriage. The authority of Benedict XIV. is foolishly invoked in favor of this opinion. This learned Pope only calls it very probable, out of consideration for the number of its adherents. But in the same work

(*De Synod. Diœcesana*) where he gives it this testimony, he affirms positively that in marriage the priest is only a witness representing the Church, in order to authorize the action of the contracting parties: *Parochus interest matrimonio tanquam testis authorizabilis pro ecclesia.* And again, as pope, in his decretal to the archbishop of Goa, he recognizes that in the action of the contractors there are all the elements of a true sacrament: *Materia est mutua corporum traditio, verbis ac nutibus assensum experimentibus, et mutua corporum acceptatio forma.*

Father Perrone judiciously exposes the dangerous consequences of the opinion of Cano and of his adherents. The greatest of all is, that this opinion can easily be made use of to establish the impious doctrine of the separation of the contract and the sacrament in Christian marriage, and so justify all the encroachments of the secular power.

(Cf. Perrone, *De Matrimonio Christiano*, Lib. i. sect. i., cap. 11).

Conference II.

(*See the first part: Unity of marriage.*)

It is certain that the intention of God in the institution of marriage was *unity* with *indissolubility*. But this intention is always veiled in the divine institution, to serve later on as the foundation of the law of Christ. At the origin of the human family there is no express law forbidding polygamy.

God might permit it, in spite of its inconveniences, because these might be overcome by the principal end of marriage, which is the propagation of the human race. Polygamy is, no doubt, fitted for the execution of the divine command given to all living creatures, "Increase and multiply, and fill the earth." And it may have been necessary during a certain time and in certain climates for the equilibrium of the sexes. "With the patriarchs," says St. Thomas, "its design was the multiplication of the race destined for the worship of God; now, as a principal end deserves more attention than a secondary end, God perhaps permitted less account to be taken during a certain time of the secondary ends of marriage, to which the prohibition of polygamy is attached, when it was more necessary to assure the principal end, that is to say, the multiplication of the people of God:" *Oportebat prædictum naturæ præceptum prætermitti ut major esset multiplicatio prolis ad cultum Dei educandæ. Semper enim principalior finis magis observandus est quam secundarius. Unde cum bonum prolis sit principalis matrimonii finis, ubi prolis multiplicatio necessaria erat debuit negligi ad tempus impedimentum, quod posset in secundariis finibus evenire, ad quod removendum præceptum prohibens pluralitatem uxorum ordinatur* (*Summ. Theol.* supp. quæst. 45. a. 2).

Did the patriarchs need a divine inspiration to believe themselves authorized to have polygamy? St. Thomas thinks so: *In hoc a solo Deo dispensatio fieri potuit per inspirationem internam* (Loc. cit.). Others think that in the absence of an express and determined law the patriarchs may have conformed to the custom, excused by the end which they had in view: the multiplication of the children of God: *Sufficiendæ prolis causa erat uxorum plurium simul uni viro habendarum inculpabilis consuetudo* (S. Aug., *De doctrin. Christ.*, lib. iii., cap. xii., n. 20).

Besides, let us remark that polygamy could not be permitted to the patriarchs except on certain conditions, which should be founded on the honesty of the end.

First, all the women should be true wives. Secondly, the first and principal wife should either expressly or tacitly cede her right.

The example of the patriarchs does not excuse infidels with whom polygamy has become a veritable debauch.

Whilst *Calvin* abuses the patriarchs and makes a crime of their polygamy, *Luther* permitted the landgrave of Hesse to have two wives at the same time; for the reason, says he, "that a Christian ought to be free to follow the example of the patriarchs." Touching agreement of two reformers who shared the same rule of faith, the sole authority of the Sacred Scriptures!

Simultaneous polygamy is forbidden in the New Law; can we say the same of successive polygamy, that is to say, of second marriages after the death of one of the partners?

The *Montanists*, imitated by the *Novatians*, absolutely condemned second marriages as illicit and execrable. Tertullian is their interpreter in his book on monogamy.

Let us remark that, although the Church has condemned this error, she has little sympathy with successive marriages. She suppresses in second marriages ceremonies which she grants as a favor to first marriages: in the Latin Church, the blessing with the veil; in the Greek Church, the coronation.

Let us remark, in the second place, that the Greek Church has shown much more severity than the Latin. Although she does not consider third and fourth marriages illicit absolutely, she has always disapproved of them as proofs of incontinency. Finally, let us remark that the Church has always manifested her preference for the state of widowhood, which she regards as a more perfect state than marriage, provided it be preserved for the love of chastity.

Having made these remarks, we should acknowledge with the Church that second marriages are perfectly legitimate. The Apostle has clearly proclaimed the right of the woman after the conjugal tie is broken by death: *Mulier.... si dormierit vir ejus, liberata est; cui vult nubat.* "He who marries when he has become a widower does not sin," says Hermas: *Qui nubit post viduitatem non peccat* (*In Pastor.*, lib. ii.). Clement of Alexandria writes exactly the same thing, always remarking that he who marries again deviates from the high perfection preached in the Gospel: *Non implet autem summam illam vitæ perfectionem, quæ agitur ex evangelio* (Lib. iii. *Stromat.*).

Some theologians have been struck by the severity with which the holy Fathers have spoken of second marriages; several have thought they condemned them as unlawful. This is an error. Cotelier spent all his erudition in proving this opinion; in all, he has only been able to bring together eleven witnesses: Athenagoras, Theophilus of Antioch, St. Irenæus, Tertullian (still Catholic), Minutius Felix, Origen, St. Gregory Nazianzen, St. Amphilochius, St. Chrysostom, St. Ambrose, and St. Jerome. But these witnesses, says Father Perrone, do not deviate from Catholic doctrine, if they are rightly interpreted. They only prove the intention of the Fathers to excite the faithful to greater perfection, by exhorting them to keep chastity in widowhood.

But if second marriages are lawful, why inflict penalties on those who remarry? They are unfit for sacred orders. Formerly, they were subjected to public penance, prayers, fastings, abstinences. They were refused the blessing of the priest; in the Greek Church the coronation was denied them. They were deprived of the alms of the Church, and their marriage was made with a sort of secrecy. This proves that the Church does not regard second marriages with a favorable eye, because they indicate a tendency to the pleasures of the flesh; but that does not mean that she condemns them as unlawful.

Although the Church regards third and subsequent marriages with far more repugnance than second ones, she does not forbid them, and her rigor of discipline in this respect is not dogmatic.

The words of the Apostle which permit remarriage after the rupture of the conjugal tie by death are general and indicate no limit to the repetition of marriage. "Men," says St. Augustine, "agitate the question of third and fourth marriages. I condemn nothing. Who am I that I should define what the Apostle has not defined?" *De tertiis et de quartis nuptiis solent homines movere quæstionem. Unde, ut breviter respondeam, nec ullas nuptias audeo damnare. . . . Quis enim sum, qui putem definiendum, quod nec Apostolum video definiisse.* "However many the number of marriages, I dare not condemn them on my own authority and without the authority of Scripture:" *Nec ex corde meo præter scripturæ sanctæ auctoritatem, quotaslibet nuptias audeo condemnare* (Lib. *De bono viduit.*, cap. xii.).

St. Jerome, the severest of the Fathers with regard to the repetition of marriage, even to calling it a prostitution or disguised fornication, protests in the following terms against those who accuse him of condemning marriage: "Let the calumniator blush who asserts that I condemn those who marry, when he has read in my writings that I condemn neither bigamy nor trigamy, nor even those who have eight successive wives. But it is one thing to condemn, another to recommend:" *Erubescat calumniator meus, dicens me prima damnare matrimonia, quando legit: non damno bigamos et trigamos, et si dici potest octogamos. Aliud est non damnare, aliud prædicare* (Epist. Ad Pammach. xlvii.). These last words of St. Jerome sum up perfectly the feeling and the conduct of

the Church with regard to those who remarry.
(Cf. Perrone, *De Matrimonio Christiano*, tome iii., lib. iii., cap. i. et ii.)

(*See ibid.: Indissolubility.*)

That marriage is indissoluble by divine law is incontestable. Is it so by natural law? One opinion, which St. Alphonsus Liguori calls very common, replies affirmatively and in absolute manner to this question. Divorce, say the partisans of this opinion, violates the equality which should exist between husband and wife; for the wife cannot withdraw from the conjugal union with the same advantages as the husband. If she provoke the rupture, she withdraws from the authority of her husband, to whom she should be subject; if the husband has the power to abandon her, her condition degenerates into a veritable servitude.

In the second place, divorce destroys the union which should exist between husband and wife; it favors ill-assorted marriages; it cools and weakens love; it is an encouragement to violent and disturbing passions, which multiply dissensions in order to get rid of a tie which incommodes them, and so to recover their liberty and the right to seek another union; it opens the road to the most shameful crimes, especially that of adultery.

In the third place, divorce is injurious to the education of children, which cannot be completed without the simultaneous concurrence of father and mother.

In the fourth place, divorce deeply troubles

families. It sows the seeds of hatred, discord, lawsuits, and becomes consequently a principle of dissolution for society.

Finally, it dishonors marriage itself, condemned to become shortly a pure concubinage, a kind of legal prostitution. We have developed all these arguments in our conference commenting on the remarkable words of the Sovereign Pontiff Leo XIII., in his Encyclical *Arcanum divinæ sapientiæ.* We should add, say the theologians whose sentiments are thus expressed, the condemnation of the sixty-seventh proposition of the Syllabus: *Jure naturæ matrimonii vinculum non est indissolubile, et in variis casibus divortium proprie dictum auctoritate civili sanciri potest.* Whence it must be concluded that indissolubility is not only conformable to natural law, but that it is commanded and exacted by natural law.

There is truth in this opinion, but the conclusion from the arguments it employs is exaggerated. If indissolubility is commanded by the natural law, it is difficult to explain the dispensation granted by God. We must have recourse to the opinion of Scotus, generally abandoned by theologians; that is to say, that God has the power to dispense from the precepts of the second table, with the exception of the one which forbids lying, or rather to explain the conduct of God by this strange supposition, that He does not dispense from a precept of the natural law by authorizing divorce, but that he uses his absolute right to break the conjugal tie, and to destroy the marriage in order that another may be contracted. These acts of authority appear to us to be not conformable to the habitual order of Providential action.

Another extreme opinion, the representatives of which, among theologians, are Sanchez, Bellarmine, Swartz, Simonnet, Lherminier, Collet, Sardagna, etc., and among Christian philosophers, Galluppi, Genovesi, Liberatore, maintains that indissolubility is not of the natural law, or at least that it is impossible to prove it by reasoning.

Far from being contrary to the principal end of marriage—the propagation of the human species—divorce may in certain cases be the only means of obtaining this end; for example, when a first marriage is sterile, especially if the sterility of one of the partners is only relative. If marriage be considered a remedy for concupiscence, it is difficult to see why divorce should not be permitted, when the incurable infirmity of one of the married pair prevents the use of this remedy. In short, if it is true that a child is more easily and better brought up by the simultaneous concurrence of father and mother, divorce nevertheless does not render its education impossible, nor compromise it more than a separation which might be perpetual. Thus the principal reason brought forward to prove that indissolubility is commanded by the natural law, that is to say, the necessity of the union of father and mother for the education of the child, is not convincing, and besides, nature, far from being repugnant to divorce, seems in some cases to demand it. Besides, the permission of divorce given by God to His people, in the Mosaic legislation, is an historical fact, which confirms this opinion. This permission would certainly not have been granted if the rupture of the conjugal tie had been contrary to the law of nature.

We should remark that the patrons of this doctrine do not pretend that the conjugal tie may be broken at will. There must be grave reasons for that, and it is well understood that the dissolution of marriage should not occasion any prejudice to the generation and early education of children.

In spite of these reservations, we do not see how, by withdrawing the natural law, they can escape the condemnation of the proposition we have quoted above: *the tie of marriage is not indissoluble by natural law, and in the different cases which occur divorce strictly speaking may be decreed by the civil authority.*

Between the two opinions which we have just explained, there is a third, which removes all the difficulties on the side of the dispensation granted by God and on the side of the condemnation of the eighty-seventh proposition of the *Syllabus*; it is the opinion of St. Thomas, adopted by Father Perrone in his treatise, *De Matrimonio Christiano* (tome iii., lib. iii., sect. ii.).

"The indissolubility of marriage," says the holy Doctor, "is of natural law:" *Inseparabilitas matrimonii est de lege naturæ* (*Summ. Theol.* supp. quæst. 57, a. 1). Nevertheless, it does not belong to the first precepts of the law of nature, but only to the second precepts, that is to say, to secondary and derived natural law, with which God can dispense for reasons drawn from nature itself. It is sufficient, for example, that, wishing to prevent a greater evil, he should permit one of the secondary ends of marriage, the education of children, to be only imperfectly attained, as happens in the case of divorce. Briefly, divorce not being immediately and directly opposed to the first intention of nature in marriage, which is the generation of children, and consequently to the first precepts of natural law, God has seen fit to permit it: *Non videtur esse contra primam intentionem naturæ demissio uxoris; et per consequens, nec contra prima præcepta, sed contra secunda legis naturæ; unde etiam primo modo (id est ex aliqua causa naturali, per quam alia causa naturali impeditur in cursu suo) sub dispensatione posse cadere videtur* (Loc. cit., a. 2).

In fact, God permitted divorce to His people to prevent those domestic crimes to which they were exposed by the hardness of their hearts: *Libellus repudii in lege permissus fuit. . . . . . propter majus malum cohibendum, scilicet uxoricidium ad quod Judæi proni erant, propter corruptionem irascibilis* (Loc. cit. a. 3). This opinion seems to us the most reasonable. It permits us to invoke the natural law against the adversaries of indissolubility, at least to justify fully the divine law, as we have done in our conference. On the other hand, it offers us an easy way to escape the objection drawn from the Mosaic law.

Conference III.

(See the first part.)

THE greater part of the philosophers of antiquity, even the most wise, denied the indissolubility of marriage, and considered divorce as perfectly legitimate: *Plato, Cato, Cicero,* as well as the jurists *Paulus, Cajus, Ulpianus,* professed the doctrine of divorce without limit.

This absolute doctrine, long forgotten since the transformation worked by Christianity in institutions and customs, has reappeared under the pen of modern philosophers and politicians. *Hennet* (1785), *Braun* (1788), *Wertsmeister, Bentham, Ferrari,* and, generally speaking, all the apostles of socialism and communism, claim the liberty of divorce. Novelists even speak philosophically on this grave question. We refer the reader to our conference, in which we have brought forward the reasons invoked by the advocates of divorce and the sad consequences of their doctrine.

Protestantism began the war against indissolubility on a less wide field. Heresy, the ill-usages capable of rendering the conjugal house uninhabitable, the unnecessary absence of one of the married pair, adultery more than all, appeared to it sufficient reasons for breaking the conjugal tie. We have quoted in the notes of our former conference the canons of the Council of Trent which condemn this error.

It is on adultery that Protestantism insists most,

because it considers itself authorized by Our Lord's words to the Pharisees: *Dico autem vobis quia quicumque dimiserit uxorem suam, nisi ob fornicationem, et aliam duxerit, mœchatur; et qui dimissam duxerit, mœchatur:* " I say to you, whosoever shall put away his wife, except it be for fornication, and shall marry another, committeth adultery, and he that shall marry her that is put away committeth adultery" (St. Matt. xix. 9). These words had already been pronounced on another occasion in almost the same form: *Ego autem dico vobis, quia omnis qui dimiserit uxorem suam excepta fornicationis causa, facit eam mœchari; et qui dimissam duxerit adulterat* (St. Matt. v. 32).

According to the Protestant interpretation Jesus Christ, while suppressing divorce in the other cases tolerated by the Jewish law, authorized it in the case where one of the married pair was guilty of adultery. This is the meaning attributed to these words: *Nisi ob fornicationem—excepta fornicationis causa.*

Catholic theologians and interpreters, in order to protect the doctrine of the Church against the attacks of heresy and schism, have given divers interpretations of the two texts in St. Matthew. We will not speak of them, for we do not consider them true.

With the Councils of Florence and of Trent we believe that Jesus Christ, in the circumstances when the words quoted above were pronounced, forbade divorce absolutely, because He proclaimed absolutely the indissolubility of marriage. If we consider only the text itself, it seems indeed as if Jesus Christ established an exception to indissolubility in the case of adultery, but the context does not permit us to adopt this opinion, because it would be placing the Saviour in contradiction with Himself.

What does Christ desire? To bring back marriage to its primitive institution. Those whom God has united are henceforth but one flesh, and man has no right to separate them. If Moses permitted divorce, it was purely by tolerance and contrary to the primitive institution. In the kingdom of Christ on earth they shall return strictly to the divine plan. This is certainly the obvious sense of the discourse of Our Lord with the Pharisees. Now all this beautiful argument falls at once, destroyed by the very word of Christ, the moment he lays down, like the Jews, the principle that divorce may exist in certain cases, contrary to natural and divine law. The words *nisi ob fornicationem* could not, therefore, apply to the tie of marriage nor establish a special case in which divorce would be permitted.

Another contradiction. On the one hand, in the first part of the text, Jesus Christ would affirm that the union is dissolved by the adultery of the wife, and that man becomes free to marry again; on the other hand, in the second part, he would forbid to marry the unfaithful wife, under the pain of adultery: *Qui dimissam duxerit mœchatur.* Thus He would suppose that the marriage tie is dissolved for the offended man, and that it is not so for the unfaithful woman, which is an absurdity. If the words *nisi ob fornicationem* imply a condition of rupture, they should have been repeated after the word *dimissam*. For example, Jesus Christ should have said : *Qui dimissam duxerit mœchatur, nisi mulier fuerit dimissa ob fornicationem.* The concession made for the case of adultery should therefore be understood as a simple separation, and not as a rupture of the conjugal tie. The decree of indissolubility therefore contains three articles:

Art. I.—A husband is not permitted to separate from his wife, except in the case of adultery.

Art. II.—Even in such a case he cannot marry another wife without himself committing adultery.

Art. III.—Whoever marries the unfaithful wife becomes guilty of the same crime.

Such was, certainly, the thought of Our Lord, and it was in this sense that His hearers understood His words. The apostles, especially, expressed their astonishment at the severity of the conditions made for marriage by the New Law, even to asking whether it were not better to abstain from marriage. They would not have been terrified to such a degree, if Jesus Christ had tolerated divorce at least in the case of the misconduct of the wife.

If we compare the text in St. Matthew with other portions of Scripture, more light is thrown on the passage, and the Catholic doctrine is confirmed. St. Mark and St. Luke speak in an absolute manner, without the slightest reference to the clause in St. Matthew. We read in St. Mark: *Quicumque dimiserit uxorem suam, et aliam duxerit, adulterium committit super eam. Et si uxor dimiserit virum suum et alii nupserit, mœchatur* (St. Mark x. 11, 12). In St. Luke: *Omnis qui dimittit uxorem suam, et alteram ducit, mœchatur; et qui dimissam a viro ducit, mœchatur* (St. Luke xvi. 18). Nothing can be plainer. Exegesis obliges us to explain the obscure passage in St. Matthew by these texts so full of precision. St. Paul is not less precise: " The woman is bound to her husband so long as he lives ; ... she is an adulteress if she has intercourse with another man during the lifetime of her husband:" *Mulier alligata est legi quanto tempore vir ejus vivit* (I. Cor. vii. 39). *Igitur vivente viro vocabitur adultera si fuerit cum alio viro* (Rom. vii. 2, 3).

As to tradition, Maldonatus sums it up in these few words: " The doctrine of the absolute indissolubility of marriage has in its favor the most ancient, the most numerous, and the best authors:" *Hæc sententia antiquiores, plures, meliores habet auctores.* We refer the reader again to the learned treatise *De Matrimonio Christiano*, in which Father Perrone demonstrates that the teaching of tradition is in perfect conformity with the doctrine of the Gospel and of the Apostle, as we have explained it. After having quoted the indisputable testimony of Hermas, St. Justin, Athenagoras, Clement of Alexandria, Origen, St. Cyprian, St. Gregory Nazianzen, St. Ambrose, St. Chrysostom, Theodoret, St. Jerome, St. Augustine, St. Innocent, of the

Council of Elvira (306), the Council of Arles (314), of the Fourth Council of Mileve (418), the learned theologian discusses the texts and standard works prior to the sixth century, on which the adversaries of absolute indissolubility endeavor to establish their opinion. He shows that the greater part of them can be interpreted in a Catholic sense, and that if some seem obscure in meaning not one of them openly admits the marriage of husbands and wives separated on account of adultery. It is, therefore, false to say that the Fathers are divided in opinion, and that the tradition of the first centuries on this question oscillates between affirmation and negation.

Certain documents of the middle ages are not less explicit. The result of their examination proves that from the sixth century the doctrine of absolute indissolubility has always been taught and practised, and has everywhere rested on the authority of the Gospel and of the Apostle, to forbid Christians marrying during the lifetime of either husband or wife even in case of separation on account of adultery.

The documents of the middle ages made use of by the adversaries of absolute indissolubility are either doubtful or badly interpreted. When they speak of the rupture of the conjugal tie it must always be understood as a simple separation, which implies no right to contract a new union.

If we can suppose that one or two provincial Councils have wrongly interpreted the text of the Gospel, and have taught that the conjugal tie was broken by adultery, we must simply conclude that they were mistaken. Their doctrine would have no weight against that of the universal Church. Besides, as Father Perrone judiciously remarks, if the meaning attributed to the text of St. Matthew by the adversaries of absolute indissolubility were the true meaning, conformable to the doctrine of the Apostle and of tradition, how does it happen that in spite of the exactions of passions and of the license granted by civil laws we have, in a doctrinal and practical point of view, a contrary meaning flowing plenteously through the course of centuries, from the origin of Christianity down to our own days?

The practice of the Greek Church, which permits, even among the United Greeks, husbands and wives separated on account of adultery to contract new marriages, is not a difficulty over which the adversaries of absolute indissolubility can triumph.

1. It is certain that the two churches of East and West were during the first centuries agreed on the interpretation of the Gospel, and no controversy was ever raised between them on the subject of the rupture of the conjugal tie by adultery.

2. This rupture was only introduced into the Greek Church after a long practice of absolute indissolubility. The reason of this is attributable to the civil laws; it was not till much later on, when they had been reproved by the Latin Church for this abuse, that the Greeks thought of appealing to the testimony of Scripture and of the Fathers.

3. The testimony of the Fathers appealed to by the Greeks is wanting in clearness, and can, for the most part, be given an orthodox meaning; in any case, it does not invalidate the frank declarations of St. Gregory Nazianzen, of St. John Chrysostom, and of Theodoret, who condemn the civil laws from which the practice of divorce has arisen.

4. The Greeks have always felt so little sustained by Scripture and tradition that they have never dared to reproach the Latin Church for her doctrine of absolute indissolubility, neither have they introduced it even among the most futile pretexts for their schism.

5. Each time there has been a question of the reunion of the two Churches, under Stephen V., under Gregory X., under Eugenius IV., there has never been any doctrinal dissent concerning absolute indissolubility.

6. The Roman Pontiffs have never ceased to reprove the Greeks for this abuse, and the Greeks have never been able to defend themselves and have never accused the Roman Church, which condemned their conduct of error, although they persevered in their course. From all this we must conclude that the error of the Greeks is rather in practice than in theory. However, since the definition of the Council of Trent it is impossible to consider this question as purely one of discipline; it is doctrinal and dogmatic.

An attempt has been made to explain away that part of the seventh canon of Session XXIV. thus rendered: "If any one says that the Church has been and is in error when she has taught and teaches, according to evangelical and apostolical doctrine, that the tie of marriage cannot be broken by the adultery of husband or wife, that a married person, even innocent, cannot during the lifetime of the partner contract a new marriage, that they commit adultery, if husband, he takes another wife, if wife, she takes another husband; let him be anathema."

Sarpi, Courrayer, Launoy, and other more recent authors assert that in this canon it is purely a question of discipline that is referred to, which the Church can change according to the exigencies of time and place, and that anathema has only been pronounced with regard to this question against the Protestants and Calvinists who dispute the Church's prerogative of infallibility. Fruitless subtilty! The Council of Trent modified its primitive formula at the entreaty of the Venetians, who demanded that the population of the Greek islands subject to their dominion might not be directly struck with anathema; but its intention manifestly was to define a dogmatic question. The terms of the canon make it a matter of faith, since it is a question of covering with the infallible authority of the Church a teaching conformable to the doctrine of the Gospel and of the Apostle: *Cum docuit et docet, juxta evangelicam et apostolicam doctrinam.* Whence we should conclude that the canon of the Council of Trent is a dogmatic canon, having for its direct object the infallibility of the Church when she teaches absolute indissolubility, and for indirect object this indissolubility taught according to evangelical and apostolical doctrine. Whoever denies the infallibility of the Church in this matter is a heretic and falls under the anathema. Whoever teaches a doctrine contrary to that of the Church on this particular point falls into error approaching heresy.

Cf. Perrone., *Tract. De Matrimonio Christiano*, sect. *De Indissolubilitate Matrimonii Christiani*, cap. ii., iii., iv.

Conference IV.

(*See first part.*)

1. WE have established the legislative power of the Church on these two principles: 1. That marriage in its essence is a sacred thing belonging to the *forum internum*, over which, consequently, the civil power has no right. 2. That in Christian marriage the contract is inseparable from the sacrament which places the conjugal union in the hands of the Church, the sole dispenser and regulator of sacred things. These principles, universally admitted in the Church, were rejected by Protestantism. We have quoted the sacrilegious comparison of *Calvin*, who places the institution of marriage on the same footing as agriculture and the most vulgar trades. "All that comes from God," says he, "and none of it is sacred:" *Non satis est matrimonium esse a Deo, ut sacramentum censeri possit ; nam etiam agricultura et ars sutoria est a Deo, nec tamen est sacramentum* (*Inst.* lib. iv., cap. xix., § 54).

Khemnitz was not long in drawing the conclusions from this error, and he asserts that it does not belong to the Church but to the civil power to make laws on marriage. But the theory of the rights of the secular power over the conjugal union was not put forth in all its impudence until theologians and court jurists sold to princes the right of establishing diriment impediments.

Luther refused this right to the Church because he only granted it to God and recognized no other impediments than those which He has established between near relations and which are particularized in the fifteenth chapter of Leviticus (*De captiv. Babyl. De matrimonio*). *Calvin, Bucer,* and *Melanchthon* are of the same opinion. But other innovators have been more daring. Mark Antony de Dominis, apostate bishop, is at the head of the flatterers who sold to the secular power the right of creating impediments to marriage. His sacrilegious doctrine has been aggravated by Launoy. This disguised Lutheran has not feared to affirm that the right of the secular power in this matter is so entirely its own that the Church cannot exercise it without usurpation, unless it is ceded to her by princes. *Jus statuendi impedimenta, quæ dirimant matrimonium, ita propria ac nativa potestate ad soles reges ac principes civiles pertinet, ut Ecclesia nequeat sine usurpatione, aut indulgentia et concessione principum illud exercere* (*De regia in Matrimonium Potestate*, 1674). Lhuillier has exposed the insincerity of Launoy, by showing in his work the numerous alterations of the texts of which he has been guilty. (*In lib. mag. Launoii Parisiensis qui inscribitur, Regia in matrimonium potestas, observationes, auctore theologo Parisiensi.*)

The error of Launoy was vulgarized in Austria by Benedict Oberhauser, professor of canon law, with this modification, that he reserves to the civil power the right of making diriment impediments because it is mistress of the contract, and concedes to the Church the right of legislating in all that regards the sacredness of the sacrament, without, however, being able to decree anything about the validity of the contract. It was on these principles that the matrimonial legislation of Joseph II. was established.

Among Catholic theologians there are some who, while recognizing that the power of creating impediments belongs originally and properly to the Church, teach that this power is shared by the secular government. Such is the opinion of Sanchez, P. Soto, Tournely, Collet, and in modern times of M. Carrière, professor at the seminary of St. Sulpice. But Carrière, in a new edition of his " Treatise on Marriage," has altered his opinion and declared his submission to the doctrine of the Holy Apostolic See.

What is this doctrine? We find it, to begin with, in the Canons of the Council of Trent, by which the Church defines that there are other impediments to marriage than those contained in Leviticus, and that she has the right to establish these impediments.

Can. III. *Si quis dixerit eos tantum consanguinei-*

tatis et affinitatis gradus, qui Levitico exprimuntur posse impedire matrimonium contrahendum, et dirimere contractum, nec posse Ecclesiam in nonnullis illorum dispensare, aut instituere, ut plures impediant et dirimant; anathema sit.

Can. IV. *Si quis dixerit Ecclesiam non potuisse constituere impedimenta matrimonium dirimentia, vel in iis constituendis errasse; anathema sit.* (Sess. xxiv.)

In vain Launoy asserts that this definition is not dogmatic, and that it does not establish a truth of the faith. It suffices to consider its object to be convinced of the contrary. The object of Canon IV. is not a fact but a law, consequently a truth. It anathematizes an erroneous *teaching* and establishes at the same time the contrary *teaching*.

Besides, the intention of the Church is manifestly expressed in the very title of Session XXIV: *Doctrina de Sacramento matrimonii;* and the Council openly declares that it desires to exterminate heresies and errors: *Hæreses et errores exterminandos duxit.*

Will it be said that the Church, in affirming her right, does not exclude that of princes? This would be to misunderstand her constant doctrine both on the preeminence of her legislation and on the very essence of marriage. We pray the reader to read again, in our conference on " The Conjugal Tie," the texts of the holy Fathers which affirm so clearly the superior authority of the Church. We add here the following words of Pope Nicholas I.: " The laws of emperors can in no way prejudice the evangelical, apostolical, and canonical laws: *Civiles imperatorum leges nullum posse præjudicium inferre evangelicis, apostolicis atque canonicis decretis.*

As to the essence of marriage, the Church considers it a sacred thing: *Matrimonium est sua vi, sua natura, sua sponte sacrum,* says Pope Leo XIII. in his encyclical *De Matrimonio Christiano.* The Council of Trent calls it a *sacrament,* and Pius IX., after having condemned the error of Nuytz, who considers the sacrament as an accessory separable from the contract, teaches that there can be no marriage among the faithful without there being immediately and at the same time a sacrament: *Inter fideles matrimonium dari non posse, quin uno eodemque tempore sit sacramentum* (Allocut., 27 Sept. 1852).

The same doctrine is taught in the encyclical of Leo XIII. Whence it follows, as we have remarked in our conference, that the right to legislate on marriage belongs to the Church: "A contract at once natural and divine," says Father Perrone, "can only be regulated by God, immediately or mediately, that is to say, by a spiritual authority as to its substance:" *Contractus naturalis atque divinus, simul cujus modi est conjugium a sua institutione. . . . A Deo solo sive immediate sive mediate, per auctoritatem nempe spiritualem, regi decet quoad substantiam suam.* Now, the diriment impediments bearing on the conjugal tie, that is to say, on the very substance of marriage, evidently belong to the Church. To grant to the secular government the right to establish them is to place a sacred thing at the mercy of a profane power, to subject divine authority to human authority.

Secondly, let us remark that the error which attributes to the secular power the right to legislate on the very substance of marriage is founded on this other error: that the contract is separable from the sacrament. Unhappily this error has authority with jurists, and it has given occasion to the detestable practice of civil marriage.

We do not intend to designate under this name the marriages which the unfaithful contract before magistrates, and which Pope Innocent III. calls *true* marriages, although they are not completely conformable to the divine law, which has raised the matrimonial union to the dignity of a sacrament: *Matrimonia vera et non rata.*

Likewise, it is not a question of unions contracted by the faithful before civil magistrates in countries where the decree of the Council of Trent has not been promulgated. These unions are at one and the same time legitimate, and true sacraments: *Matrimonia vera et rata.*

We wish to speak of marriages contracted before the civil authority in countries where the decree of the Council of Trent, which exacts for the validity of the sacrament the presence of the proper minister, has been promulgated. In these marriages there is no contract; modern governments regard them as legitimate unions, to which they grant all civil effect; but they are in reality only shameful and sad concubinage. *Præter sa-*

cramentum, conjunctionem cujuscumque, etiam civilis legis vi initam, nihil aliud esse nisi turpem ac exitialem concubinatum ab Ecclesia tantopere damnatum (Allocut. Pii IX. ad cardinales, 27 Sept. 1852).

We do not refuse to the civil power all right of regulation with regard to marriage, but this right cannot be exercised on the very substance of the matrimonial union. To verify by a public act the formation and existence of the conjugal tie, to establish certain conditions in order that marriage may obtain its civil consequences, is the right of the secular power; but to assert that persons are legitimately married by a magistrate without the concurrence of the spiritual power is an error against which the Church protests with all the strength of the sovereign power over the very substance of marriage which God has conferred on her.

Thirdly, in virtue of her sovereign power, the Church has the right to judge all matrimonial causes which concern the very substance of the conjugal union. *Mark Antony de Dominis, Launoy, Tamburini, Litta, Nestius, Nuytz,* attribute this right to the secular power. The canon by which the Church defines her right does not exclude, say they, that of civil tribunals. The Council of Trent, indeed, expresses itself thus: *Si quis dixerit causas matrimoniales non spectare ad judices ecclesiasticos, anathema sit* (Sess. xxiv., can. 12). In these terms it condemns those who refuse to the Church the right to judge matrimonial causes, but not those who assert that this right is shared by the civil power; for the Council does not say: *Ad solos judices ecclesiasticos.*

To those who compare the canon we have just quoted with the doctrine of the Church on the identity of the contract and the sacrament, it is evident that the Council had no need to exclude civil judges, because they can have no kind of right over a sacred thing. But the Sovereign Pontiff Pius VI. has dissipated all doubts on the subject in his letter of Sept. 17, 1787, *ad Episcop. Motulensem.*

He there speaks as supreme judge of the doctrine: *Tanquam is qui jus habet suprema Christi ipsius auctoritate sibi collata docendi et confirmandi;* and he declares that the right defined by the Council belongs to the Church *alone*, which has received from God the dispensation of the sacraments; that it is false to say that the Council has not excluded the civil power, although it has not made use of this expression, *ad solos judices ecclesiasticos;* that the spirit and reason of ecclesiastical legislation exclude all idea of exception and limitation. Finally, he cites these remarkable words of the jurist Van Espen : *Unanimi consensu receptum est causas sacramentorum esse mere ecclesiasticas, easque quantum ad substantiam eorum, ad judicem ecclesiasticum private spectare, nihilque circa eorum validitatem et invaliditatem judicem sæcularem posse decernere, eo quod hæc natura sua sint mere spirituales. Et sane si quæstio versatur de validitate ipsius matrimonii, solus judex ecclesiasticus est competens, ipseque solus de hac quæstione cognoscere potest* (*Jus. eccles.*, p. iii., tit. ii., cap. i., n. 4, 11 et 12).

Thus the invalidities or separations pronounced by the civil judges can only regard the civil consequences of marriage. The conjugal tie itself and the rights it creates belong to the *forum internum* of conscience and to the sole cognizance of the Church.

Fourthly, how far does the power of the Church extend over the conjugal tie? If she can create impediments which oppose its formation, can she break it when it is formed? The answer to this question is not difficult if it refers to marriage consummated by the carnal union of husband and wife. It is certain that the Church cannot dissolve it.

As to marriage conformable to the divine law, and which is called marriage ratified and not consummated, it is of faith that it can be dissolved by solemn religious vows. The Council of Trent has defined this truth in Canon VI. of Session XXIV: *Si quis dixerit matrimonium ratum non consummatum, per solemnem religionis professionem alterius conjugum non dirimi; anathema sit.*

This canon is directed against Protestants, who by a singular contradiction, whilst showing themselves ready to divorce, even when it is a question of consummated marriage, absolutely refuse the rupture of the conjugal tie when it is a question of embracing a more perfect life. The Jansenists have imitated the Protestants in this, and have pretended that the definition of the Council of Trent is contrary to Scripture and to tradition. This is affirmed by Léridant in his " Examination of Two

Questions on Marriage" (p. 458 seq.). Pite, in his "Dissertion on the Absolute Indissolubility of the Conjugal Tie," pretends that the decree of the Council of Trent is void, because the Fathers had not the necessary liberty in publishing it.

As to Catholic theologians, they all consider the canon of the Council of Trent as the definition of a truth of the faith; but their opinions differ when they explain why marriage simply ratified can be dissolved by the profession of religion.

Some, such as the theologians of Salamanca, Bellarmine, Habert, Drouin, etc., under the leadership of St. Thomas, appeal to natural law. It should always be permitted, says the Angelic Doctor, to pass from a less to a more perfect state. The benefit of children does not suffer from it, because the marriage is not consummated; not the honor of the woman, because she keeps her virginity; nor the natural rights of the married pair, equal in this matter on one side and the other. Before the consummation of marriage there is between husband and wife only a spiritual tie. Now, this spiritual tie can be broken by spiritual death, as the carnal tie is broken by physical death: *Ante carnalem copulam est inter conjuges tantum vinculum spirituale; sed post etiam est inter eos vinculum carnale. Et ideo, sicut post carnalem, ita per ingressum religionis, vinculum, quod est ante carnalem copulam, solvitur; quia religio est quædam mors spiritualis, qua aliquis sæculo moriens vivit Deo* (*Summ. Theol.*, supp., quæst. 61, a. 2).

Others, such as Kugler, Antoine, Simonet, La

Luzerne, Pothier, under the leadership of Suarez, advocate purely and simply the ecclesiastical law. The rupture of the conjugal tie in the case in question is the application to bind and to loose, which Christ has confided to His Church. To these two opinions grave difficulties can be opposed; therefore Sanchez, Pontius, Tournely, Billuart, Collet, and nearly all modern divines, supported by the great authority of Benedict XIV., appeal to the divine law. In promulgating the law of indissolubility, Christ, they say, has made one reservation. The two texts containing His reply to the Pharisees must be placed side by side: *Jam non sunt duo sed una caro,* and *quod Deus conjunxit homo non separet.* This means to say that the indissolubility of the conjugal tie is only absolute when man and woman have become one flesh by the consummation of marriage. Such is the interpretation of the Church.

Protestants and Jansenists in vain appeal to Scripture. They have no right to determine its meaning according to their private opinion. This right belongs only to the Church. Her traditional practice and her definitions are the rule of our faith.

Fifthly, the question of the rupture of marriage ratified presents more difficulties on account of other grave reasons besides the profession of religion. Sanchez gives a long list of ancient theologians who refuse to the Sovereign Pontiff the right of dissolution, and he says of their opinion that it is the most probable. Among modern theologians, Pontius, Sylvius, Tournely, Drouin, Collet, and others, have embraced this opinion.

But we must remark that the arguments they use to prove it are partly the same as those which heretics use and abuse against the decree of the Council of Trent. Further, they are obliged to acknowledge that many times, during many centuries, the Sovereign Pontiffs have dissolved the ties of marriage before its consummation, without protestation on the part of the Church. In denying that they had the right to do so, are they not condemned by this general principle, which may be considered an axiom: " To doubt the power of the Pope after he has dispensed, is a kind of sacrilege; for it is reproaching Christ with not having provided what is necessary for the government of His Church:" *De pontificiis potestate, postquam dispensavit dubitare, instar sacrilegii est. Est enim Christo quasi exprobrare quod non satis Ecclesiæ suæ providisset* (Tit. *De convers. conjug.*, cap. vii.).

We must consider as true the opinion of theologians, who, with Suarez, Bellarmine, the school of Salamanca, Kugler, and nearly all canonists, teach that the Pope has the right to dissolve marriage before its consummation for grave and just causes. There is nothing more precise than the declarations of Benedict XIV. on this question: *Cessat quoque indissolubilitas* MATRIMONII RATI *in aliis omnibus casibus extra professionem religiosam, in quibus Summus Pontifex, justis et gravissimis causis, censet ejus dissolutionis esse locum, ita suadente Tridentino, ita exposcente observantia, ita demum convincente con-*

tinuata plurium sæculorum praxi sedis apostolicæ, ex quibus interpretatio juris divini optime colligi potest (Quæst. canon., q. cxlvi., n. 36).

Nullam de potestate summi Pontificis moveri amplius posse quæstionem in eo, quod attinet ad dispensandum super matrimonio rato et non consummato, cum hodie opinio affirmativa sit communis inter theologos et canonistas, et in praxi recepta, uti notorium est (Ibid. quæst. cccclxxix.).

Before so great an authority it would be rash to maintain the first opinion. (Cf. Perrone, Tract. *De Matrimonio Christiano*, lib. iii., cap. v., *De dissolutione matrimonii rati non consummati*.)

CONFERENCE VI.

(See the first part.)

FROM the origin of Christianity we have seen virginity flourishing in the Church. St. Justin and Athenagoras, whom we have quoted, testify to the eagerness with which a great number of Christians embraced continence. We may add to their testimony that of Clement of Alexandria, Tertullian, Origen, and St. Cyprian. This multiplication of a chaste race in the midst of a corrupt society was a strange thing for the heathen world, where it was so difficult to obtain the continence of a few priestesses, even by loading them with gifts and honors and suspending over their heads the most terrible threats. They found it difficult to understand the mysterious attraction which could induce so many persons of both sexes to sever themselves from the pleasures of the flesh. Apologists made use of it to show the excellence of Christianity, capable of producing so great a wonder. Soon they saw themselves obliged to defend virginity against the attacks of heresy. A monk, *Jovinian*, after having passed some years in a monastery at Milan, dedicated to the practice of an austere life, under the guidance of St. Ambrose, became disgusted with his condition, and, like all apostates, began to cry it down. He taught, amongst other errors, that virginity was not more perfect than marriage, and began to insult the model of virgins, the most holy Mother of Christ. Passing from Milan to Rome, he had a great number of followers. Many persons, who till then had lived in continence and mortification, renounced a kind of life which they were told was unprofitable for their salvation and perfection, married, and gave themselves up to an effeminate and voluptuous life.

Jovinian was condemned by Pope Siricius and by a Council of Milan, presided over by St. Ambrose, in the year 390. St. Jerome, in his writings against the heresiarch, speaks with all the vehemence of his dialectics and of his style to such a degree that he was accused of condemning marriage. The holy doctor showed that his ideas had been badly interpreted and expressed himself more exactly.

Protestants, heirs of the error of Jovinian, have renewed against St. Jerome the reproaches of the disciples of heresy, and have pretended that he contradicts himself. But as Bergier justly remarks, to unsay or retract what one recognizes to have been badly expressed is not a contradiction. If heretics were sincere enough to do the same, far from blaming, we should applaud them. St. Jerome is not in this position (*Dict. de theol.*, art. *Jovinianists*).

Protestantism, not content with republishing the reproaches of the Jovinianists against St. Jerome, has attacked the early Christians and the Fathers who taught them, asserting that they were mistaken. Luther in this has been surpassed by his disciples. The patriarch of the Reformation appealed against celibacy and virginity to the law of multiplication; but since then it has been found that the zeal of Christians for this holy state arose from a false prejudice of the most pernicious fanaticism, that it was an error engrafted on other errors. It arose, they say, from a stupid admiration for all that demands effort; from an ambition to be distinguished and to receive honors; from the rivalry of sects which then divided Christianity, especially of those who admit two principles, one good, the other evil; from the melancholy produced by climate; from the desire to refute the false accusations of the heathen; from the system of the pre-existence of souls; from the opinion of the Neo-Platonists, who maintained the necessity of continence and mortification in order to be united to God.

Nothing can be more frivolous or more foolish than these assertions. 1. To admire the effort of virtue which seeks to establish the empire of the soul over the flesh is not at all so stupid a thing; it seems to us far more stupid not to be impressed by it. 2. The retired life of virgins scarcely resembles ambition for honors, and everybody knows that the principal virtue recommended by those who directed them was humility, which they considered the first rampart of chastity. 3. It was not at all by a spirit of rivalry that the first Christians embraced virginity, since the first heretics claimed to be the enemies of the flesh. Virginity favored their error. 4. The melancholy of climate is a new discovery. It would prove that all climates are melancholy, because there have been virgins in all countries. 5. Even if Christians should have wished by the practice of continence to confound the heathen who accused them of revolting impurity, what harm would there have been? It was much the best way of refuting the calumny. 6. It is ridiculous to consider virginity as a consequence of the belief in the pre-existence of souls. Why practise virtue from a motive derived from an error condemned by the Church, when there is within our reach a dogma taught by the Church which sufficiently explains the generous efforts of the soul devoted to protest by chastity against the original corruption of nature? 7. For more than a century St. Justin, Athenagoras, and others had rejoiced over the multitude of virgins, celibates, religious, and ascetics, which Christianity had produced in all classes of society; when Neo-Platonism made its appearance, Hermas, Tertullian, and St.

Cyprian, the apologists of virginity, were strangers to this school and founded their doctrine on Scripture. Whence it follows that this last hypothesis, dear to Moshein and Bruker, is pure imagination.

Physiologists and economists have discussed this important and delicate question. Heresy has been reinforced by them. If we believe them, the state of celibacy and virginity is a state contrary to nature and to the interests of society.

Contrary to nature, because those who condemn themselves by a vow to absolute continence undertake to struggle against one of the most imperious temptations of the flesh, and become either prevaricators or consumptives. Happily this assertion is not a scientific oracle for conscientious physiologists. A man who has resolved never to drink wine can become accustomed to this privation, and is certainly less exposed to drunkenness than one who drinks and finds it good. The flesh exacts in proportion to what it receives. With the libertine, his appetites become insatiable.

Such is the case of the shameful celibacy which in our conference we have delivered up to the contempt of honest men. To discipline the flesh by temperance, to carry temperance to austerity, is to assure the empire of the soul over the body and elevate one's self above those imperious needs of which physiologists, the enemies of continence, make such a bugbear. If you add to austerity prayer and grace, which occupy a large place in virginity, it is hard to see why the man or woman who is bound by the vow of chastity should fatally become prevaricators. Those who assert this are people who encourage the desires of the flesh instead of preventing them. As to the consumption which may result from absolute continence, it is pure imagination, against which the ideas of the most illiterate, the constant experience of physiology, and the figures of statistics protest.

There are in the human body organs essential for the support of life which cannot relax their actions without the entire organization being shattered to its very foundations. It is the same with the nervous system, which extends its empire both over the life of relation and over that of nutrition; for it communicates life and animation to the whole system. But there are organs whose activity is limited. They can possibly suspend their functional activity without the general life suffering much from their inaction.

The degradation of mind, the exhaustion of body with which continence is menaced in the name of science, are denied by science. She finds in continence a source of energy and vigor for organic as well as for intellectual life.

Statistics agree with physiology. It is true that according to certain calculations the average of life in celibacy is below that of married people; but in these calculations are included all who do not marry, whatever their constitution or their habits. Putting aside those whose natural infirmities condemn them to celibacy, those who shirk the duties of marriage to indulge without reserve in libertinage, and only considering those who out of love for virtue embrace the state of virginity, the average of life is raised. It has been proved that anchorites lived to an average of 76 years, priests and religious of both sexes, from 58 to 63 years.

In the learned work of Doctor Duffieux, "Nature and Virginity," will be found technical details on this interesting question which I cannot give here. But I cannot resist the pleasure of quoting the beautiful letter written by Père Lacordaire to this author to thank him for the gift of his book.

Toulouse, July 31,1854.

"SIR:—I have read your work, "Nature and Virginity," and I hasten to testify to you my satisfaction. You have supported with arguments drawn from science a thesis morally evident, but which passion will attack to the end of the world, and you have done so with a clearness, moderation, prudence, and talent, which I sincerely admire. In spite of the necessary technical details, it seems to me that your book cannot offend a pure heart. You have said what was needful to be understood by learned men, and your science has remained sufficiently chaste to instruct without peril, it appears to me, those who are not initiated in the mysteries of the human body.

" You have furnished my conviction with proofs of which it was ignorant, which personally are useless to me, but which will enlighten minds more sensitive to scientific demonstration than to reasons drawn from experience and from moral order, which, also, you have not neglected. It is an eminent service rendered to a virtue which is the very basis of the regeneration of humanity. Humanity is raised or lowered in proportion as continence increases or decreases among men; it is the principle of all faith, of all strength, of all incorruptibility, and a people who loses it cannot escape from decay and servitude. How can this virtue be a crime against nature? It is incontinence which is contrary to nature, the consequence and the punishment of sin, the most horrible disorder bequeathed to the human race, and an evident mark of its degradation.

"It is not true to say that continence is difficult for the greater part of our species. Women, you have remarked, generally support it with a facility honorable to themselves, and which is explained by the very sensitiveness with which they are gifted. The more loving the heart, the less it seeks the pleasures of the body, and reciprocally the more chaste the body, the more delicate and tender the heart becomes. I have never met with a loving young man among those who give way to the debauches of the imagination and the senses.

"Women are not the only ones to whom continence is easy. I have often been astonished at how little was needed to withdraw a young man from depravity. Flight from bad companions, leaving off dangerous reading, a sober life, serious work, a continual practice of prayer, confession, Communion, and works of charity, suffice to transform hearts which thought themselves incurable; and those who are not cured, or only slightly, owe it to an idle life, full of pleasure. There may be exceptions belonging to natural temperament; but I am convinced that a great number of men would live easily in absolute continence if they lived after a Christian manner.... The longevity of priests and of religious sufficiently testifies that this virtue, which is a principle of the spiritual life, is also a most admirable hygienic measure for the body.

"You have said all this, sir, much better than I, and I only add the testimony of my experience to the authority of your scientific deductions.

"Accept my thanks for your beautiful and excellent work as well as the homage of my sincere regard.

I have the honor to remain, sir, your most humble and obedient servant,

"F. H. D. LACORDAIRE."

Economists reproach celibacy and virginity with being contrary to the interests of society. We have replied to this reproach in our conference by remarking that there are many ways of being fecund, and that the service of the multiplication of the species can be largely compensated in society by other domestic and public services.

Nevertheless, economists assert that celibacy and virginity arrest the increase of the population. May we be permitted to ask them if it would not be more appropriate to find fault with libertinage? Here is the true cause of the arresting and falling off which are considered the sinister precursors of the decay and ruin of nations. Suppress what is evidently immoral before you attack a virtue which by its example elevates the standard of morality, and contributes more than is thought to the multiplication of species and to the health of generations. We consider we are able to affirm that among the nations who know how to obey the law of God in marriage and in its calls to the special state of celibacy and virginity, the population, far from decreasing, increases in a wise proportion. Celibacy and virginity maintain a necessary equilibrium, and their service of devotedness has precisely the design of remedying the miseries from which families that are too numerous suffer. And again, economists should agree among themselves. Enemies of virginity, they accuse it of diminishing life, and on the other hand they complain of the excess of life.

Marriage is respectable only when it obeys the law of God; and conscience teaches us that, if its fecundity must be measured, it should be by a virtue, and not by an execrable vice.

ANALYTICAL TABLE OF CONTENTS.

I.—THE SANCTITY OF MARRIAGE.

First, in its primitive institution by God, the Creator of humanity; secondly, in its exaltation by Christ, the author of the sacraments.—I. Universal marriage in nature; it is full of venerable mystery; these mysteries increase with life.—Marriage of our first parents.—This is a typical marriage; we must consider its essence, for to this fundamental truth are allied the most important questions of the rights and duties of which we shall speak.—Marriage is the most exalted, the most venerable, the most peculiar of contracts in its object, its end, and its motive.—Nevertheless, this contract is not the very essence of marriage. —What is this essence?—What powers concur for the formation of the conjugal tie?—How is this tie sacred by its own strength, naturally and of itself? —II. Nature has made marriage a holy thing; it is a still more holy thing if we consider the dignity of the sacrament.— A glance of what marriage would have been in a state of innocence.—How it was depraved in the course of centuries. — How Jesus Christ came to restore it.—How the apostles accomplished His design.—The doctrine of marriage deposited for the instruction of all Christian generations in the epistles of St. Paul.

—Teaching of tradition, doctrine of the Church on marriage.—In what this sacrament consists.—Who are its ministers?—How the sacrament continues in the conjugal tie. What is the grace it produces?—Conclusion: Marriage is a holy thing.—Men must not touch it irreverently, . . . pp. 7–34.

II.—THE CONJUGAL TIE.

The conjugal tie is the very essence of marriage; it is a sacred tie in itself, become more sacred by the institution of the sacrament; a tie which is not divided, a tie which is not broken; such are its properties studied in these two propositions:—First, the indissoluble unity of the conjugal tie is a divine law; secondly, this law is in nature a law of progress and of perfection.—I. How God manifests His will in the typical marriage of our first parents; how His law, not express and imperious as it will become later on, is respected by the generations sprung from the primitive pair.—Tolerance of God with regard to polygamy and divorce; the reasons for this tolerance.—The tolerance of God with regard to the nations of antiquity does not cause Him to forget His first design in the institution of marriage. How unity and indissolubility are strengthened and asserted by the facts and teaching which shall cement the Christian restoration to the primitive institution.—How Jesus Christ restores the indissoluble unity of the conjugal tie, and how He makes it the law of the new world which He has redeemed. —Triumph of this law in the Church until the appearance of Protestantism.—How the Council of Trent has decided the dogmatic formula of the law and has placed it under the protection of anathema.—Reasons for this law published by Christ: —it was, first, His right as Creator; secondly, His right as Redeemer; thirdly, His right as Benefactor; fourthly, His right as Exemplar.—Conclusion: The law should be respected, even were there not seen in the world of nature any aspiration, any law which may justify its holy austerity; but nature gives to this law its full acquiescence, for it is a law of progress and of perfection. —II. What we understand by nature.—God having created man perfect and master of the world, it was suitable that he should be distinguished in the generating act by the most perfect of all unions: this union is indissoluble marriage.—The law of the indissoluble unity of marriage is a law of progress and of perfection: 1. Because it is the law suited to true love;—developments.—2. Because it is a school of virtue;—developments;— 3. Because it is the cement of the family and the honor of human society:—developments.—Apostrophe to the pretended men of progress.—The men of progress are the apostles and faithful observers of the indissoluble unity of the conjugal tie. . . . . .pp. 35–60.

III.—DIVORCE.

IN this conference is shown the counter-proof of the truths already explained.—The adversaries of the divine law agree with us on the progressive character of monogamy, and on the disadvantages and inconveniences of polygamy.—It is very different when it is a question of the indissolubility of the conjugal tie, which they pretend is a tyrannical law, that must be replaced for the alleviation of modern society by the faculty of divorce. We will show: 1. That the reasons appealed to against the divine law are incapable of shaking it;—2. That divorce, by which they desire to replace this law, is worse than all the evils for which they hold indissolubility responsible, and that it is for human society a principle of decay.—I. Character of general laws.—They should not be abrogated on account of their inconveniences.—Examination of the grievances invoked by the adversaries of the divine law against the indissolubility of marriage: 1. The law of indissolubility outrages human liberty, which it enchains even to slavery.—Reply—2. The law of indissolubility tends to frustrate the principal end of marriage.—Reply—3. The law of indissolubility exposes those whom it irrevocably unites to being unjustly and hopelessly deprived of the happiness to which they have a right on entering into conjugal society; it exasperates and urges them to crime.—Reply.—II. Divorce is worse than all the evils for which they would make indissolubility responsible, and is consequently a principle of decay.—Beautiful and powerful words of Leo XIII. on this subject.—Everything suffers from divorce: 1. Marriage itself.—2. Those who marry.—3. Children, families, the whole of society.—Developments.—How easy it is to understand after these developments that divorce is a principle of decay.—To those who accuse us of making here a case of a tendency, we reply by history: 1. Divorce in antiquity.—2. Divorce in Christian society since the appearance of Protestantism.—If divorce become the habit of our society, our decay will be deeper and more shameful than any historical decay, because we shall fall from a greater height.—The necessity for true Christians and sensible men to proclaim, in their manners more than in their discourse, that we cannot separate what God has joined, ...pp. 61–87.

IV.—LEGISLATION ON MARRIAGE.

PRETENSION of the secular power to reply to the demands of the adversaries of the divine law; it desires that marriage should be the concern of the State before being the concern of any Religion and any Church; it desires that the laws and regulations of religious society should bend before the laws and regulations of the State. 1. Against this pretension of the secular power it is established that the legislation on marriage as to its essence and its essential properties belongs to God alone and to His Church.—2. This truth proved, it is shown with what wisdom and with what power the Church proceeds in her matrimonial legislation.—I. Refer to the truths explained in the preceding conferences with regard to the essence of marriage.—The principle laid down, that all the strength, all the reason of marriage is in the tie formed between man and woman by the mutual giving and accepting of their persons; that this tie is marriage itself, and it is always God who makes it. This is shown thus: 1. That the secular power has no right over what is given in marriage; 2. That what man makes by giving himself does not concern it; consequently, that marriage, even outside the Christan ordinance, is, as to its essence and fundamental properties, subject to the law of nature and the law of God, and is independent of all civil law.—The incompetency of the secular power is still more manifest if we consider that marriage is a sacrament.—Inseparability of the contract and the sacrament.—Marriage being chiefly a sacred thing, the civil power can have no authority over its essence and its fundamental properties.—What the limits of the legislative power of the secular government with regard to marriage are.—The essence, the intrinsic properties, the tie of marriage transformed and elevated by Christ, can only proceed from a sacred authority.—This authority is the Church.—Detail of her power.—II. The Church, invested with a sacred power, after the manner of legislators worthy of the name, knows how to unite wisdom and force in the preventive, merciful, and avenging measures which she takes to protect and establish the venerable institution of matrimony.—1. Wisdom.—The philosophy of impediments.—All the Church's legislation on this point is made in the interests of liberty—of the multiplication and health of human generations—of social unity—of the security and peace of the domestic hearth, of the purity of faith, of the rights of God and the rights of man—of the honor and good reputation of marriage itself.—Developments.—2. Force.—The courageous and persevering resistance of the Church has triumphed : 1. over the opposition of the laws ;—over the licentiousness of the great.—Consequences of this resistance.—The Church has saved the holy cause of matrimony, ... pp. 88-114.

V.—THE PROFANATION OF MARRIAGE.

It is shown in this conference that the greater number of those who complain of the divine law only suffer from it because they have outraged it and have made it for themselves the chastisement of a profanation.—Three great benefits of marriage : *Proles, Fides, Sacramentum*—that is to say : children, the sweets and consolations of faithful intimacy, the grace of the sacrament.—How these three great benefits are profaned.—I. Fecundity is a blessing from God; He has promised it to those whom He loves.—Spectacle of the family where children multiply.—How the Christian who understands this blessing knows how to enter into the designs of God, and prepares with a profound respect for himself for the honor of paternity.—How, on the contrary, there are miserable men who profane the first benefit by the premature exhaustion of their own life.—Another more common profanation is the crime of those who limit their paternity.—How God avenges this crime.—His chastisements are due to profaners, not only because they have offended God and cheated nature, but because they have betrayed their country.—Developments.—II. What fidelity is.—How the wise man, the Christian, will make sure of this possession, of this great benefit.—Manner in which Christian husband and wife prepare for marriage.—They enter by the door of wisdom; they remain under the guard of fidelity.—How, on the contrary, with a number of persons, interest, vanity, frivolity, insincerity are the too common agents of matrimonial unions.—Is it astonishing that infidelity installs itself where everything conspires against the benefit of fidelity? and if they complain of being crushed under the inflexible yoke of the conjugal tie, whose fault is it?—III. Grace of the sacrament.—Efficaciousness of this grace to correct the imperfections of nature.—Who are they that receive this grace?—Sad, cruel, perilous unions of young girls, who ally their faith with indifference or incredulity.—How they are chastised for having lent their aid to the profanation of a sacrament.—If such are the marriages in which the sacrament is only partially profaned, what must they be when the profanation is complete.—The sacrileges which are committed in the exchange of vows.—How man and woman bring down upon themselves the curse of God instead of His grace.—If they are unhappy after that, they are punished wherein they have sinned.—Conclusion of these considerations.—Appeal to young persons, ... pp. 115–137.

VI.—CELIBACY AND VIRGINITY.

According to certain too fervid interpreters of the law of multiplication, this law is obligatory on all the world; it is a disgrace not to have fulfilled it; it is a crime voluntarily to withdraw from it.—To these advocates of marriage at all costs we demonstrate: 1. That the state of celibacy and virginity is a state desired by God; 2. That it is one of the most beautiful and most useful ornaments of Christian society.—I. How the slow and progressive march of God is remarked in the preparation of the matrimonial law, and also in the preparation of the evangelical counsel which requires from certain privileged souls a nobler and more perfect state than marriage.—The traditions of humanity.—How they should be understood.—Apparition of the virgin Christ.—When He fixes the legislation of marriage, He declares His desire to draw virgins to Himself and assign them a special place in His kingdom.—Interpretation of this desire by the apostles.—Abundant germination of virginity in Christian society.—The holy Fathers, their apologies for virginity.—Conduct of the Church.—Her doctrine on the state of celibacy and virginity.—The Church proclaims that it is better and happier to remain a virgin than to marry.—She is right.—II. A general glance over the vast field of regenerate humanity, the domain of God.—He has a right to reserve certain portions of this domain.–What are these reserved portions?—Shameful celibacy and morose virginity do not belong to the reserved portions of God's domain.—The virgins whom God desires, whom He knows and loves, are those whom He has touched with His grace, and who, responding to His loving advances by a free choice, have become: 1. the copies of His perfection; 2. Angels of the earth;—3. The spouses of Christ:—4. The living Gospel.—Developments of these privileges and characteristics of virginity.—Evidently, they place us in the presence of one of the most beautiful ornaments of Christian society.—It is a useful ornament.—Three great services of virginity: 1. the service of example, 2. the service of prayer, 3. the service of devotedness.—We understand why the Church asks from her priests celibacy, why she cultivates virgins lovingly.—All the virgins whom God loves are not in convents, and those whom the despising voice of the world calls old maids shall be proud and avenged when, in presence of the whole world, Christ shall call them His spouses.—Canticle of Wisdom in honor of virginity, ... pp. 138-168.

INDEX.

Index of the principal errors contrary to the dogmas set forth in this volume, ... pp. 169-222.

www.ingramcontent.com/pod-product-compliance
Lightning Source LLC
Chambersburg PA
CBHW021819230426
43669CB00008B/803